WORLD WAR II

WRITTEN BY
R.G. GRANT

LONDON, NEW YORK,
MELBOURNE, MUNICH, AND DELHI

For Toucan Books:
Senior editor Jane Chapman
Editor Caroline Saltissi
Editorial assistants Hannah Bowen, Amy Smith
Senior designer Thomas Keenes
Designers Mike Cornwell, Ralph Pitchford,
Steve Woosnam-Savage

For Dorling Kindersley:
Consultant Terry Charman
Senior editors Victoria Heyworth-Dunne, Claire Nottage
Senior art editor Jacqui Swan
Managing editor Linda Esposito
Managing art editor Diane Thistlethwaite
Publishing manager Andrew Macintyre
Category publisher Laura Buller
Picture researcher Louise Thomas
Cartographers Ed Merritt, John Plumer
Production editor Andy Hilliard
Jacket editor Mariza O'Keeffe
Jacket designer Natasha Rees
Jacket design manager Sophia Tampakopoulos-Turner
Production controller Angela Graef
DVD research consultant James Barker
DVD producer Brian Holmes
US editor Margaret Parrish

First published in hardback in the United States in 2008
This paperback edition first published in 2011 by
DK Publishing, 375 Hudson Street, New York, New York 10014

Copyright © 2008 Dorling Kindersley Limited

Produced in association with the Imperial War Museum, London, England
www.iwm.org.uk

11 12 13 14 15 10 9 8 7 6 5 4 3 2 1
WD173 – 02/11

A catalog record for this book is available from the Library of Congress.

Hardback edition ISBN: 978-0-7566-3830-6
Paperback edition ISBN: 978-0-7566-7325-3

Color reproduction by Colourscan, Singapore
Printed by Toppan, China

Discover more at www.dk.com

IMPERIAL WAR
MUSEUM

WORLD WAR II

the events and their impact on real people

WRITTEN BY
R.G. GRANT

END GAME

THE AFTERMATH

CONTENTS

*I*T IS VITAL *that each new generation of young people should learn about the titanic global conflict of World War II. The war affected the lives of everyone around the globe and, more than any other single event, it shaped the world that we inhabit today.*

The pages that follow aim to bring the drama and tragedy of the war vividly to life through a wide range of illustrative material, and also through the testimony of people who were there. While giving a balanced record of the course of military events, the book also brings into sharp focus the experience of wartime for the ordinary individual.

This unique account explores the impact of the war worldwide, including often neglected areas, such as the plight of the civilian population of India and other Asian countries. The climactic moments of the war, including the D-Day landings and the dropping of the atom bombs on Hiroshima and Nagasaki, are covered in depth, but everyday life at war is also thoroughly explored—from rationing and occupation by a foreign army, to popular wartime movies and songs.

This book is an ideal supplement to school studies of World War II, but more than that, it provides an opportunity for young people to understand the struggles of their grandparents and great-grandparents in a past that can seem remote to children today, but is, in reality, very recent.

FOREWORD

THE ROAD TO WAR

WORLD WAR II WAS a huge conflict that had a devastating effect on the whole world. The war resulted from the rise of dictators—new, ruthless politicians who were able to take power because the world had been destabilized by World War I and by economic depression. Italian dictator Benito Mussolini, Adolf Hitler in Germany, and Japan's military leaders were prepared to resort to force to achieve their goals.

Nazi parade
Nazi Party banners, bearing the slogan "Germany awakes," are carried at a rally in Nuremberg, in Germany, in 1933. Led by Hitler, the Nazis took Germany into a campaign of aggression and expansion against its neighbors that led directly to war.

July 28
Austria-Hungary declares war on Serbia and World War I begins

July 29
Adolf Hitler becomes leader of the Nazi Party in Germany

November 9
Hitler fails to overthrow the German government by force in the Munich *Putsch*

April 6
The United States declares war on Germany

November 11
Germany is forced to agree to an armistice, ending World War I

January 10
The League of Nations meets for the first time

October 28
Mussolini is installed as head of government in Italy

January 3
Mussolini takes dictatorial powers in Italy

| 1914 | 1917 | 1918 | 1919 | 1920 | 1921 | 1922 | 1923 | 1925 | 1929 |

August 4
Britain declares war on Germany

February 23
Benito Mussolini forms the first Fascist Party in Italy

January 1
The Soviet Union is established

October 24–29
The collapse of share prices on the New York Stock Exchange (the Crash) marks the start of a worldwide economic depression

November 7
A revolutionary Bolshevik (communist) government takes power in Russia

June 28
The Versailles Peace Treaty is signed. Most Germans regard the peace terms imposed on them as unfair

August 2
Hitler becomes *Führer*
(dictator) of the
German Third Reich

December 13
Japanese troops massacre
hundreds of thousands of people
in the Chinese city of Nanking

August 23
Nazi Germany and the Soviet
Union sign a pact secretly agreeing
to divide Poland between them

September 14
Elections to the German parliament
show that Hitler's Nazis have
become a party with mass support

November 8
Franklin D. Roosevelt
wins the US
presidential election

October 3
Italy invades Ethiopia.
The League of Nations
fails to take action

July 7
Japan invades
China

September 29–30
At the Munich Conference,
Czechoslovakia is forced to give
its Sudetenland region to Germany

1930	1931	1932	1933	1934	1935	1936	1937	1938	1939

September 18–19
Japanese troops invade
Manchuria, northern China

March 16
Hitler announces that Germany
is building up its armed forces,
forbidden by the Versailles Treaty

March 11
German troops march into
Austria, which becomes part
of Germany on March 13

May 22
Germany and
Italy sign the
Pact of Steel

January 30
Hitler becomes chancellor
(head of government)
of Germany

March 7
Hitler moves troops into
the Rhineland, contrary to
the Versailles Treaty

July 17
The Spanish Civil
War begins and
lasts until 1939

September 1
Germany invades Poland.
Britain and France declare war
on Germany two days later

9

THE GREAT WAR AND THE PEACE TREATY

THE GREAT WAR OF 1914 TO 1918, later known as World War I, was a huge conflict fought mostly in Europe. It cost at least 10 million lives and ended with the defeat of Germany. Most people hoped that such a terrible war would be "the war to end all wars," and that it would be followed by a lasting peace. But many Germans regarded the peace treaty signed in 1919 at Versailles, in France, as deeply unfair. They were left feeling angry and resentful.

Trench warfare
In World War I, France, Britain, Russia, Italy, and the US fought against Germany and Austria-Hungary. Soldiers on both sides suffered terrible conditions in the trenches. Troops were killed by machine-gun fire, explosive shells, and poison gas. They were also plagued by rats and lice, and, due to the unclean conditions, were vulnerable to diseases.

Peace conference
US President Woodrow Wilson (right), French leader Georges Clemenceau (centre), and British Prime Minister David Lloyd George met in Paris in 1919 to draw up a peace settlement. Wilson dreamed of a democratic Europe where disputes were settled peacefully through a League of Nations. But Clemenceau wanted to weaken Germany to protect France from future attack, and Lloyd George followed his tough line.

Bitter Germany
The experience of the Great War was especially bitter for the Germans, who were forced to surrender in November 1918. Millions of German soldiers had been killed, wounded, or taken prisoner. Many Germans refused to accept the defeat, claiming that their army had been "stabbed in the back" by disloyal German politicians and revolutionaries.

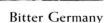

Versailles Treaty

The terms of the peace treaty were decided by the victors, and Germany was forced to accept them. The Germans were especially upset by a "war guilt" clause that blamed them for starting the Great War. It stated that the Germans would have to make massive "reparation" payments, mainly to Britain and France. In addition, Germany was only allowed to keep a small army, it lost territory, and parts of the country were occupied by foreign troops.

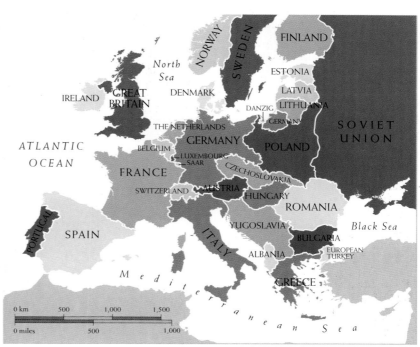

New map of Europe

The Great War radically altered the map of Europe. New nations were created—Poland, Yugoslavia, Czechoslovakia, Finland, Estonia, Latvia, and Lithuania. The Austro-Hungarian Empire collapsed and became the separate states of Austria and Hungary. Germany lost an eighth of its prewar territory, much of it to Poland. German losses included Alsace and Lorraine, which the Germans had taken from France in 1871. The former Russian Empire became the Soviet Union (USSR), but lost land to Poland and the new Baltic states.

Worthless money

In 1923 the German government decided it could not afford to pay reparations. As a result, France and Belgium sent troops into Germany to take what they believed they were owed. German money lost almost all its value through "hyperinflation." A huge pile of 100,000 German marks (seen here) had the same value as just one US dollar. Germans blamed these troubles on the Versailles Treaty.

LEAGUE OF NATIONS

The League of Nations, the forerunner of today's United Nations, held its first meeting in 1920. There were 42 founder members. The goal of the League was to solve conflicts by negotiation, rather than by war. Member nations were to unite against the nation that had broken the peace. Unfortunately, the United States never joined the League because the US Congress feared it would drag America into more foreign wars. Initially, Germany and the Soviet Union were not invited to be members, although Germany did eventually join in 1926.

11

Italian Fascism

Benito Mussolini fought as a soldier in World War I. After the war he created the Fascist movement, dressing its followers in uniforms like an army. He promised to bring order, national unity, and military glory to the country. His policies appealed to many Italians who were worried about a possible communist revolution, and were angry that Italy had not benefited from the war, despite being on the winning side.

FASCISM AND NAZISM

BRITAIN, FRANCE, AND THE UNITED STATES—the main victors in World War I—were democracies, with elected governments and laws protecting the freedoms of individual citizens. But in many countries in the 1920s and 1930s, movements opposed to democracy and individual freedom took power. Italy was one of the first countries to come under the rule of a dictator—Benito Mussolini, leader of the Fascist Party. Economic collapse and mass unemployment gave Adolf Hitler, leader of the Nazi Party, an opportunity to overthrow democracy in Germany.

Hitler and Ludendorff

After fighting in World War I, Adolf Hitler became leader of the Nazi Party in July 1920. In 1923, along with German war hero General Ludendorff (left), he led an attempt to seize power in Germany by force. But police opened fire on the Nazis and the *putsch* failed. Hitler was tried, found guilty, and imprisoned for nine months.

Tough rule

Mussolini came to power in Italy in 1922 after his Fascists threatened to stage a "march on Rome." Once installed, he gradually abolished parliamentary democracy and created a dictatorship—a state ruled by a leader with total authority. At the time, many Italians were pleased to have a strong government that maintained order and promised a glorious future. Those who disagreed were silenced. Even children were enrolled into Fascist organizations, which taught them it was good to wear uniforms and to admire Mussolini.

Mein Kampf

The publicity surrounding his trial made Hitler famous. While in prison he wrote his autobiography, *Mein Kampf* ("My Struggle"). The book set out his belief that Germany needed to overthrow the Versailles Treaty and to win *lebensraum* ("room to live") by conquering the "inferior" Slav peoples of eastern Europe. Hitler also denounced the Jews as an evil people responsible for Germany's downfall.

Swastika

Many young unemployed men joined Hitler's Nazi movement. They became his Stormtroopers—uniformed thugs who beat up his political opponents. They wore the Nazi symbol of the swastika as an armband.

By January 1933 there were around six million unemployed in Germany, almost one in three working people.

Mass unemployment

In the mid-1920s the German economy recovered from the effects of World War I, helped by money that flowed in from the prosperous United States. During this time, Hitler won little support. But in 1929, a worldwide economic depression began, bringing widespread unemployment. Voters flocked to support extremist parties, especially the Nazis and the communists. Election posters like this one told the German people that Hitler was their "last hope."

Hitler becomes chancellor

Between 1930 and 1932 there were three elections to the German parliament. An astonishing public speaker, Hitler blamed all Germany's woes on the Versailles Treaty and promised that a Nazi government would make Germany great again. By 1932 Hitler was the most popular political leader in Germany, but the Nazis failed to win an overall majority in parliament and Field Marshall Hindenburg became president. But in January 1933, Hitler was made chancellor—head of the German government.

Rearmament

Hitler rejected the part of the Versailles Treaty that limited Germany's armed forces. He withdrew Germany from the League of Nations and from disarmament talks. He was very eager to rebuild the *Luftwaffe*, the German air force, as quickly as possible, using vast factories to manufacture aircraft.

NAZIS IN POWER

AS HEAD OF THE GERMAN THIRD REICH (Nazi dictatorship between 1933–1945), Hitler set about crushing the opposition. All political parties except his Nazi Party were banned, and its opponents were arrested. When the German president, Hindenburg, died in 1934, Hitler declared himself *Führer* ("leader"). He built up the army with the goal of creating a "Greater Germany" that would include the territory lost after World War I.

Himmler's SS

The SS ("protection squad") was the most feared organization in Nazi Germany. Run by Heinrich Himmler, it controlled the secret police (the Gestapo) and ran the concentration camps in which they locked up anyone seen as an enemy, such as Jews and communists. The SS showed their elite status by wearing black uniforms and shiny boots and carrying fancy daggers.

Uniformed spectacle

The Nazis staged spectacular propaganda events, such as annual rallies in Nuremberg, to create the impression of a nation united. Packed ranks of uniformed Germans gathered to show their adoration of the *Führer*, who inspects them from a balcony.

RACIST STATE

The Nazis were racists who, from the early days of Nazi rule, mercilessly victimized German Jews. Laws were passed making it illegal for Jews to work in many jobs, and Germans were discouraged from having themselves treated by Jewish doctors or buying goods from Jewish-owned stores. Books by Jewish authors were burned. Sometimes Jews were publicly humiliated, forced to do degrading work while their German neighbors watched, or cruelly paraded through towns in carts.

23.9.1933 Erster Spatenstich
23.9.1936 1000 km Autobahn fertig

The Nazis created the Hitler Youth to prepare children for their future role as soldiers. Hitler wanted a generation of "victorious, active, daring youth, immune to pain."

onquering unemployment

e Nazi regime was popular in its early rs because it brought unemployment to end. People found jobs in armaments ories or in the fast-growing army, and Nazis also created work through ding *autobahns* (highways). Hitler had self photographed digging the first leful of dirt for an *autobahn*.

Hitler Youth

From the beginning, the Nazis put special phasis on teaching the young their view of he world. Young Germans were enrolled in Hitler Youth movement and were taught to lize the *Führer* and hate the Jews. Children ere encouraged to inform the authorities if their parents criticized the Nazi regime.

15

"German and Italian rearmament is proceeding much
more rapidly than rearmament can in Great Britain…
In three years Germany will be ready for war…"

Adolf Hitler, 1936

Nuremberg, Germany—A huge crowd of SS soldiers stands to attention, listening to Hitler speaking during a Nazi Party rally

WEAKNESS OF THE DEMOCRACIES

BRITAIN AND FRANCE, the major European democracies, reacted feebly as Nazi Germany tore up the Versailles Treaty and Fascist Italy became more aggressive. The democracies were determined to avoid war at all costs and actually felt that Germany had been harshly treated. Some British and French politicians even welcomed the strength of Nazi Germany, hoping Hitler would defend Europe against the communist Soviet Union. As the League of Nations failed to take action against Fascist aggression, the dictators seemed to hold all the best cards.

Antiwar feeling
By the 1930s antiwar feeling was very strong in Europe and the United States. *All Quiet on the Western Front*, a book and film powerfully condemning the war, were hugely popular. In a debate at Oxford University in 1933, British students declared they would not fight for "king and country." Even Hitler had to pretend to be a man of peace in public in order to keep popular support in Germany.

Prophet of war
Winston Churchill, a Conservative member of the British parliament, warned of the threat of German aggression and called for Britain to re-arm. At first he was dismissed as a warmonger, but he was later commended for accurately foreseeing the Nazi menace.

America neutral
The United States was too busy coping with problems caused by the Depression to worry about Europe. The US Congress passed Neutrality Acts banning the president, Franklin D. Roosevelt, from involving America in foreign wars in any way.

Popular Front
In 1936 the Popular Front, a socialist government that was supported by French communists, came to power in France. Led by Léon Blum, the Popular Front wanted a stronger stand against Hitler and Mussolini. But France was bitterly divided. Some people even said they preferred Hitler to Blum.

ДА ЗДРАВСТВУЕТ ВОЖДЬ НАРОДОВ
ВЕЛИКИЙ СТАЛИН—ТВОРЕЦ КОНСТИТУЦИИ
ПОБЕДИВШЕГО СОЦИАЛИЗМА И ПОДЛИННОГО ДЕМОКРАТИЗМА!

Stalin and the Soviet Union

The Soviet Union, which included Russia, Ukraine, and Belarus, could have been a vital ally in the fight against Hitler. But Soviet leader Joseph Stalin had created a communist dictatorship that during the 1930s killed hundreds of thousands of its own people. As a result, British and French leaders disliked Stalin as much or more than they disliked Hitler. Stalin returned the compliment, seeing both Hitler and the democracies as enemies of communism.

Forming the Axis

Fascist leader Mussolini was irritated that Britain and France opposed his invasion of Ethiopia, even if they did nothing practical to stop it. In November 1936, he signed a treaty of friendship with Hitler. Germany and Italy became known collectively as the Axis powers.

Italy invades Ethiopia

In 1935 Fascist Italy invaded Abyssinia (Ethiopia), an African country that was a member of the League of Nations. The League half-heartedly imposed sanctions against Italy, but they were soon lifted and Italy was able to conquer Ethiopia in seven months.

THE SPANISH CIVIL WAR

Franco
The rebel forces, known as the Nationalists, were led by General Francisco Franco. He had the support of much of the army, the Catholic Church, and the Falangists—the Spanish equivalent of the Fascists and Nazis.

In July 1936, generals in the Spanish army rebelled against the democratic government of the Spanish Republic, starting a civil war that would eventually cost around 400,000 lives. Nazi Germany and Fascist Italy took the chance to try out their armed forces in support of the rebels. The Soviet Union intervened on a smaller scale, backing the Republic. But France and Britain did nothing, dooming the Republic to defeat in 1939, when Spain became a dictatorship under General Franco.

Condor Legion
The Nazi German forces, sent to aid General Franco, were known as the Condor Legion. They consisted mostly of aircraft, including *Junkers* Stuka dive-bombers, with a small number of tanks and anti-aircraft guns. Fighting in Spain made German pilots the most skillful and experienced in Europe.

International Brigades
About 60,000 foreign volunteers traveled to Spain to defend the Republic against Franco, and to join what they saw as a worldwide struggle against Nazism and Fascism. Volunteers were formed into International Brigades, such as the "Commune of Paris" battalion, which was made up of French and British volunteers.

Around 10,000 Spanish people were killed in bombing raids during the Spanish Civil War. The vast majority of these were victims of the German Condor Legion.

Prisoners massacred
Brutal massacres were common on both sides throughout the civil war. More than 100,000 Republican soldiers and civilians captured by Nationalists during the war were shot dead by their captors.

Guernica
On April 26, 1937, Condor Legion aircraft bombed Guernica, in northern Spain. Much of the town was destroyed and around 1,600 civilians were killed. Suddenly, anti-Facist literature and artwork appeared in Spain. The scale of the devastation gave a frightening indication of German air power. It made people in Britain believe that in a war with Germany, London and other cities would be quickly destroyed.

Nationalist triumph
After the Nationalist victory in March 1939, hundreds of thousands of Republicans were imprisoned by Franco or fled across the Spanish border to France. The triumphant Nationalists staged victory parades in Madrid and other Spanish cities, cheered on by supporters giving Fascist salutes.

China divided
By the 1930s, Chiang Kai-shek (left) was the leader of the Chinese Nationalist government, but he only ruled part of the country. His authority was rejected by local warlords and by the communist followers of Mao Ze Dong. Chinese weakness tempted Japan to act.

Manchuria occupied
In 1931 Japanese troops occupied Manchuria, part of China. China appealed to the League of Nations for help in resisting this act of aggression, but the League did nothing. Japan put P'u Yi in place as a puppet governor of the state of Manchuria, known as "Manchukuo."

WAR BEGINS IN THE EAST

WHILE THE SITUATION IN EUROPE WORSENED, Asia erupted into all-out war. Since the late 19th century, Japan had been the only non-Western major military and economic power. Although much larger than Japan, China had fallen into a chaotic state that left it vulnerable to attack. After gradually moving in on Chinese territory for years, Japan launched a full-scale invasion in July 1937. The Japanese army occupied much of China, but failed to achieve a final victory.

Sacred emperor
Although Japan's Emperor Hirohito was worshipped by some Japanese people as a god, in practice the country was dominated by its armed forces. General Hideki Tojo, the army chief of staff, argued that Japan should conquer Asia in preparation for a "race war" against the white peoples of the West. Although the emperor was basically peace-loving, he often appeared in uniform, for example, when inspecting the giant listening devices intended to give Japan forewarning of approaching enemy aircraft.

ANTI-COMINTERN PACT
In 1936 Japan signed the Anti-Comintern Pact with Nazi Germany. The pact was based on a shared hostility to communism. The Japanese wanted German support against the Soviet Union, which had claims to Manchuria. The link between these two countries was to prove vital during World War II, by connecting Japan's war in Asia and the Pacific to Germany's European war.

Battle for Shanghai

After the Japanese invasion of China in July 1937, some of the most intensive fighting broke out in the major port-city of Shanghai, witnessed by Americans and Europeans. Chinese troops determinedly held out for three months, battling for every house and street, while large areas of the city were destroyed by Japanese bombing. The bravery of the Chinese resistance was a huge shock to the Japanese invaders.

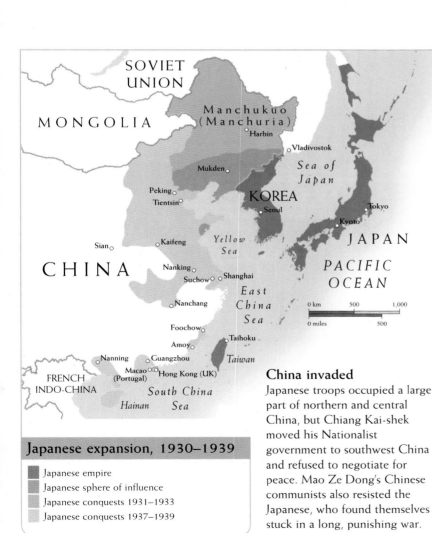

Japanese expansion, 1930–1939

- Japanese empire
- Japanese sphere of influence
- Japanese conquests 1931–1933
- Japanese conquests 1937–1939

Attack on Nanking

The Japanese army entered the city of Nanking in December 1937. In the weeks that followed, their soldiers were responsible for atrocities on a massive scale. Some estimates claim as many as 300,000 Chinese were ruthlessly massacred.

China invaded

Japanese troops occupied a large part of northern and central China, but Chiang Kai-shek moved his Nationalist government to southwest China and refused to negotiate for peace. Mao Ze Dong's Chinese communists also resisted the Japanese, who found themselves stuck in a long, punishing war.

Empires under threat

France, Britain, and the Netherlands ruled large parts of Asia, and the United States ran the Philippines. Japanese expansion was a severe threat to these interests. The British were building a new naval base in Singapore, defended by impressive-looking guns, which the men are seen here cleaning, but they knew they couldn't take on the Japanese if they were fighting a war in Europe at the same time.

HITLER WINS WITHOUT WAR

BETWEEN 1936 AND 1938, Hitler completed the overthrow of the Versailles Treaty and expanded Germany's borders. This increase of German power was achieved without a shot being fired. Britain's Prime Minister Neville Chamberlain gambled on a policy of "appeasement," hoping that Hitler would be satisfied if he was allowed to take over German-speaking areas around his borders. But Hitler wanted much more.

Rhineland occupation

The Versailles Treaty banned the Germans from stationing troops in the Rhineland, the part of Germany bordering France and Belgium. In March 1936 Hitler took a huge risk and sent soldiers into the Rhineland. If Britain and France had responded with military force, Hitler would have had to withdraw because Germany was not yet ready for war. But the democracies did nothing.

Anschluss with Austria

In March 1938, Hitler used a political crisis in Austria to justify sending troops in to take over the country. Most Austrians welcomed the *Anschluss* ("link-up") with Germany and Hitler was given a warm reception when he drove through the Austrian capital, Vienna. But Austria's large Jewish community was immediately treated with brutality.

German expansion, 1936–1939

- Germany at the beginning of 1936
- Territory gained by the end of March 1939

North Sea

DENMARK

Baltic Sea

MEMEL
(Incorporated into Third Reich, March 1939)

FREE CITY OF DANZIG

LITHUANIA

THE NETHERLANDS

o Hamburg

GERMANY (EAST PRUSSIA)

POLAND

o Berlin

BELGIUM

GERMANY

Breslau

RHINELAND DEMILITARIZED ZONE
(Reoccupied March 1936)

LUXEMBOURG

SUDETENLAND
(Incorporated into Third Reich, October 1938)

o Prague

FRANCE

Nuremburg o

PROTECTORATE OF BOHEMIA AND MORAVIA
(Incorporated into Third Reich, March 1939)

o Stuttgart

LIECHTENSTEIN

o Munich

Vienna o

SLOVAKIA

SWITZERLAND

AUSTRIA
(Incorporated into Third Reich, March 1938)

ITALY

HUNGARY

YUGOSLAVIA

0 km 100 200 300
0 miles 100 200

German expansion

The German takeover of Austria and the border areas of Czechoslovakia, described here, took place in 1938. The following year the Germans took over the rest of Czechoslovakia without a fight. Germany also seized Memel from Lithuania.

Sudeten Germans

After the *Anschluss*, Hitler focused on the Sudetenland area of Czechoslovakia. The Nazis stirred up protests by Sudeten Germans, who claimed they were being mistreated by the Czechoslovak government. Hitler began preparations for a war with Czechoslovakia.

Chamberlain and appeasement

As Hitler increased his pressure on Czechoslovakia, British Prime Minister Chamberlain decided to negotiate face-to-face and met the Nazi leader in Berchtesgaden, in Germany. Chamberlain's policy of "appeasement" meant he was prepared to pressure the Czechs into giving way. But the more concessions were made, the more Hitler demanded.

Preparations for war

Hitler remained determined to seize Sudetenland, and France and Britain realized appeasement had failed. The democracies began preparing for war in late September, building defensive trenches to protect against air attack, which was expected to be swift and utterly devastating.

Munich Pact

At the end of September 1938, Mussolini initiated a conference in Munich between Britain, France, Germany, and Italy, in a last-minute bid to avoid war. The Czechs were betrayed by their allies and forced into accepting all of Hitler's territorial demands. Czechoslovakia was left defenseless.

"Peace for our time"

Chamberlain made a triumphant return from Munich with a signed statement of friendship between Britain and Germany. On his arrival back in England he paraded this piece of paper around, claiming to have successfully achieved "peace for our time."

COUNTDOWN TO WAR IN EUROPE

THERE WAS WIDESPREAD RELIEF when the Munich agreement kept the major European powers at peace in 1938, but the slide to war soon resumed with a vengeance. The Nazis' brutal treatment of Jews threw doubt on the idea that Hitler was a political leader who could be trusted. After the Germans occupied Prague in spring 1939, Britain and France committed to defending Poland, the next probable target of Nazi aggression. Hitler knew that the result of attacking the Poles would be war with Britain and France.

Kristallnacht

On November 9–10 1938, Nazis burned synagogues—Jewish places of worship—and attacked Jewish businesses across Germany. The night became known as *Kristallnacht* ("Night of Broken Glass").

Czechoslovakia destroyed

In March 1939, Slovakia became a separate pro-German state and the German army occupied the rest of Czechoslovakia, marching unopposed into the capital, Prague. Finally convinced that Hitler's expansion could only be stopped by the threat of war, Britain and France promised to support Poland and Romania if Germany attacked.

After Kristallnacht, around 30,000 Jews were rounded up and sent to concentration camps.

American Neutrality

US President Roosevelt condemned the *Kristallnacht* atrocities. He was very concerned at the rise of Nazism, but his hands were tied by a series of Neutrality Acts passed by Congress, which strictly banned any involvement in foreign wars.

Pact of Steel
Although Mussolini invaded Albania in April 1939, he knew his forces were not fit for a war with Britain and France. In May he signed an alliance with Germany called the Pact of Steel, but he tried to persuade Hitler to keep from starting a general European war.

Nazi-Soviet Pact
Britain and France needed an alliance with Stalin's Soviet Union to defend Poland. But the democracies were reluctant to deal with the communist dictator. Instead, Hitler negotiated a "non-aggression" pact with Stalin—up to that point his most bitter enemy.

The Polish corridor
Danzig was a city on the Baltic coast with a German population. It was at the top of the strip of land through Germany that gave Poland access to the Baltic Sea. When the Poles refused to allow Danzig to become part of Germany, Hitler had his excuse to invade Poland.

Declaring war
German troops invaded Poland on September 1, 1939. British Prime Minister Chamberlain and French Premier Édouard Daladier still hesitated to act. But Chamberlain reluctantly declared war on Germany on September 3, and France followed suit.

GERMANY TRIUMPHANT

THE FIRST TWO YEARS OF THE WAR were a triumph for Nazi Germany, which conquered most of Europe in a series of lightning military campaigns. With its main ally France defeated, Britain, led by Winston Churchill, fought on—although British cities were heavily bombed. When Italy joined in the war the fighting spread to the Mediterranean and the North African desert. In June 1941, Hitler invaded the Soviet Union and his armies advanced to the gates of Moscow. But despite huge losses, the Soviet people battled through.

Balkan invasion
During Hitler's Balkan campaign of 1941, Yugoslavia was occupied between April 6–17. Here German troops are seen advancing into a village in Serbia, then part of Yugoslavia.

November 30
The Soviet Union invades Finland, starting the Winter War, which ends in March 1940

April 9
Germany invades Denmark and Norway, ending the "Phoney War"

July 10
In the Battle of Britain, which lasted until October 1940, the Royal Air Force stops the *Luftwaffe* from gaining command of the air

September 1
The evacuation of thousands of British children begins

May 10
Over a four-day period Germany invades Belgium, the Netherlands, Luxembourg, and France

June 10
Italy declares war on Britain and France

September 3
The US gives Britain 50 destroyers in return for a lease on British naval and air bases

1939

1940

September 27
Warsaw surrenders after four weeks of war

May 10
Winston Churchill becomes British Prime Minister

June 22
France surrenders to Germany

March
Soviet dictator Joseph Stalin orders the execution of some 20,000 Polish prisoners

May 27–June 2
Allied forces are evacuated by sea from Dunkirk

September 7
The Blitz begins. *Luftwaffe* bombers carry out air raids on London and other British cities until May 16, 1941

January 5
British forces in the North African desert drive the Italians out of Egypt and invade Libya

April 6
German forces invade Yugoslavia and Greece

September 8
The Soviet city of Leningrad (St. Petersburg) is put under siege. The siege doesn't end until January 27, 1944

November 5
US President Roosevelt is reelected for a third term

February 13
General Erwin Rommel and the Afrika Korps arrive in North Africa

May 27
The German battleship *Bismarck* is sunk in the Atlantic

July 12
Britain and the Soviet Union sign a mutual agreement to fight together against Nazi Germany

1941

November 14
Coventry suffers devastating bombing from the *Luftwaffe*

May 20
German airborne forces are dropped on the Mediterranean island of Crete, which falls to Germany

August 9–12
Churchill and Roosevelt meet off Newfoundland and agree to the Atlantic Charter

September 29–30
More than 30,000 Jews are murdered by the Nazi SS at Babi Yar outside Kiev

November 11
British carrier aircraft sink Italian warships in harbor at Taranto

March 11
President Roosevelt signs the Lend-lease Act, which allows the US to supply Britain with war goods without payment

June 22
Hitler launches Operation Barbarossa, a massive invasion of the Soviet Union

December 5
The German advance in the Soviet Union is halted by a Soviet counterattack in front of Moscow

THE DEFEAT OF POLAND

WHEN THE GERMANS INVADED POLAND in September 1939, Britain and France did nothing to help their Polish allies. Even before the Soviet Union joined in by attacking the country from the east, the Poles had no chance of resisting the invasion. They were forced to surrender after just four weeks' fighting. Germany and the Soviet Union divided Poland between them. Whether ruled by the Nazis or the Soviets, Poland's inhabitants suffered mass murder, starvation, and exploitation as slave labor. The country's large Jewish population was almost totally wiped out by the Nazis.

BLITZKRIEG

With the invasion of Poland, Germany tried out a new style of hard-hitting, fast-moving warfare. This *Blitzkrieg* ("lightning war") relied on attacks by aircraft, such as Stuka dive-bombers, to terrorize the enemy, while columns of tanks and trucks smashed their way through weak points in defenses and drove deep into enemy territory. These shock tactics were astonishingly successful in the first two years of the war.

Whirlwind Attack
The Germans invaded Poland on September 1, 1939. Although German soldiers are seen here cheerfully removing frontier barriers, the invasion was brutal. German aircraft attacked Polish airfields, guns fired on troops, and tanks surged across the border.

Polish cavalry
The Poles were poorly equipped compared to the Germans. The Polish army depended on horses for transportation. Most of the German army also depended heavily on horse-drawn transportation, but the Germans had far more aircraft and tanks than the Poles.

Bombardment of Warsaw

German forces surrounded the Polish capital, Warsaw. Trapped, the city's population was bombed by German aircraft and shelled by German artillery. The Poles held out bravely under this bombardment, but the situation was hopeless. Polish military commanders surrendered Warsaw to the Germans on September 27.

More than 6 million Poles died in World War II—one-fifth of the population.

Polish Jews

There were more than 3 million Jews living in Poland. The Nazis forced Polish Jews to move into areas known as "ghettos" and to wear identification marks, such as a Star of David. Thousands of Jews soon began dying—from starvation and mistreatment. In 1942, the Nazis set out to kill every single Polish Jew.

Katyn massacre

When the Soviet Union took eastern Poland, they captured thousands of prisoners. More than 20,000 Poles were massacred by the Soviet secret police and buried in mass graves. One of these graves was found by the Nazis in the Katyn Forest in 1941.

Poles in exile

Many Polish soldiers escaped from Poland and went to Britain and France to continue the fight against Germany. Inside Poland, the Home Army organized resistance against the Nazis. General Wladyslaw Sikorski headed a Polish government-in-exile in London. He died in a plane crash in 1943.

THE PHONEY WAR

WHEN BRITAIN AND FRANCE DECLARED WAR on Germany in September 1939, most people expected that cities such as London would be devastated by bombing within days. But this did not happen. For the first seven months of the war, the British and French hardly fought the Germans at all, except at sea. British troops were sent to France, but the Allies stayed on the defensive, waiting for Hitler to attack. Americans called it the "Phoney War."

Ready for air raids

Expecting the *Luftwaffe* to bomb its cities, Britain introduced air-raid precautions. There was a "blackout" to prevent lights from guiding bombers onto targets at night. With no street lights or headlights, lots of people died in car accidents in the pitch blackness. Everyone was issued with a gas mask because the Germans were expected to drop bombs with poison gas.

Children evacuated

Hundreds of thousands of British children were evacuated from cities to areas considered safe from bombing. They had very mixed experiences. Some were happy to move from city slums to the countryside that they had never seen. Others were traumatized by living with strangers in an odd new environment. When the bombing did not happen, many evacuees returned home.

THE MAGINOT LINE

During the 1930s, France built the Maginot Line—a vast concrete structure intended to defend the country against a German attack. The Line ran the length of France's border with Germany, but left the border with Belgium unprotected. The French hoped that by staying on the defensive they would avoid the kind of heavy losses they had suffered during World War I.

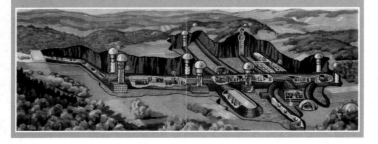

Civilians become soldiers

Through the first fall and winter of the war, Germany, Britain, and France tried to build up their forces for the battles that lay ahead. All had systems of conscription, calling up millions of civilians to put on uniforms and train to fight. Factories made guns and aircraft as fast as they could. British troops crossed to northern France, lining up alongside the much larger French army.

Ireland stays neutral

Irish leader Éamon de Valera kept his country neutral even though it was a member of the British Commonwealth. Other Commonwealth countries—Canada, Australia, New Zealand, and South Africa— all declared war on Germany, although South Africans were deeply divided on the issue.

Royal Oak sunk

From the start of the war, the Germans showed how devastating their U-boats (submarines) could be against British merchant ships and warships. In October 1939, a U-boat sank a Royal Navy battleship, HMS *Royal Oak*, in harbor at Scapa Flow in the Orkneys, off Scotland. More than 800 of the ship's crew were killed. The U-boat's commander, Günther Prien, became a war hero in Germany.

The British government distributed 38 million gas masks during the first six months of the "Phoney War."

Battle of the Plate River

In December 1939, the German pocket battleship *Graf Spee* was attacked by three Royal Navy ships in the Plate River estuary, off Uruguay. Trapped, it was later sunk by its own crew. This success boosted the popularity of Winston Churchill, who had joined the government as head of the Admiralty.

WARS IN THE NORTH

THE NAZI-SOVIET PACT of August 1939 had made the Soviet Union and Germany allies. Through the winter and spring of 1939–40, the two countries strengthened their positions. The Soviet Union invaded Finland and forced the Finns to hand over territory. Then Germany occupied Denmark and invaded Norway. Although Britain and France sent troops and warships to defend Norway, the Norwegians were defeated in two months.

Soviet invasion
Soviet dictator Joseph Stalin decided to take over some border areas of Finland, to improve his country's defenses on the Baltic. Soviet troops invaded Finland at the end of November 1939. Although the Finnish army was hopelessly outnumbered, at first it halted the Red Army. France and Britain admired the Finns for bravely fighting off the giant Russian "bear" and even made plans to send troops to help them.

Winter War
The Finns were experts at fighting in winter weather. Their ski troops moved silently, wearing white to blend in with the snow. But in the end they were beaten by the sheer size of the Soviet forces. Without help from Britain and France, Finland made peace in March 1940.

German airborne invaders
Denmark and Norway were both neutral countries. Denmark did not have enough troops to resist the Germans and was taken over in a single day, on April 9, 1940. But Norway was a tougher target. While German ships landed soldiers at Norwegian ports, airborne troops parachuted in to capture key airfields—the first paratroopers ever used in war. The *Luftwaffe* used the captured airfields to dominate the skies over Norway.

Sea battles at Narvik, April–June 1940

The British thought the strength of the Royal Navy would enable them to defend Norway. British warships sank nine German destroyers at the northern Norwegian port of Narvik. But the *Luftwaffe* aircraft bombed navy ships. Although the German navy suffered heavy losses, the Royal Navy also lost many ships to air attacks.

Scandinavia and the Baltic in 1940

German re-occupation of Memel (March 1939) and Danzig (September 1939)

German invasion and occupation of Poland (September 1939)

Soviet annexation of eastern Poland, 1939

Soviet annexation of Baltic countries, 1940

Soviet annexation of Finnish territory, 1940

→ German advance

→ Soviet advance

→ Finnish advance

→ Allied movements

— Boundary between German and Soviet spheres of influence

Outfought by the Germans

When British and French troops landed in Norway, they were poorly equipped and badly organized. Almost one in four of the Allied soldiers was killed, wounded, or taken prisoner. The last Allied troops were evacuated in early June 1940.

Scandinavia and the Baltic in 1940

Capturing Denmark and Norway boosted Germany's position in the North Sea and the Baltic. The Soviet Union took land from Finland and took over the Baltic states—Estonia, Lithuania, and Latvia—without a fight, in June 1940. Sweden stayed neutral throughout the war.

Churchill becomes prime minister

In Britain there was outrage at the failure in Norway. Prime Minister Neville Chamberlain was blamed for the situation and forced to resign. His colleague Winston Churchill, a man who had shown more warlike spirit, was asked to form a government in his place.

Quisling

Vidkun Quisling was a Norwegian who admired the Nazis and did not oppose the German invasion of his country. He later headed a government in Norway that collaborated with the German occupiers. "Quisling" became a word used in Allied countries for any traitor who sided with the Nazis.

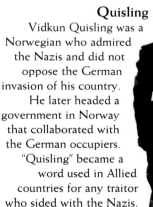

Dutch defeated

German forces invaded the Netherlands, Belgium, and Luxembourg on May 10, 1940, using airborne troops to capture airfields and key points in the defenses. The Dutch surrendered five days later after the port of Rotterdam was devastated by *Luftwaffe* bombers.

Battle for France, 1940

Battle for France, 1940

German tanks swept north to the coast, cutting off Allied troops who had advanced into Belgium. The Maginot Line was bypassed completely. France was in their sights, and would soon be at their mercy.

Battle for France

→	German advance
——	Front line, May 16
- - -	Front line, May 21
········	Front line, May 28
-·-·-	Front line, June 4
-··-··-	Front line, June 21
——	Maginot Line

ATTACK IN THE WEST

IN MAY 1940 THE GERMAN ARMY LAUNCHED its long-awaited offensive in Western Europe. The Germans combined tanks and aircraft with deadly effect in a war of rapid movement that utterly defeated the slower-moving Allies. In less than a month, the British had been forced to evacuate their army from Dunkirk, and the French were in hopeless disarray.

German panzers

German tanks ("panzers") were neither more numerous nor larger than British or French tanks, but they were used much more effectively. German tanks advanced in strict formations while the Allies' tanks were scattered in support of infantry. The Germans advanced quickly, not waiting for the rest of the army to catch up.

Civilian refugees
French and Belgian civilians fled from the scene of the fighting with all the belongings they could carry. Thousands of horse-drawn carts and cars clogged the roads, blocking the movement of Allied troops. The refugees were also bombed and shot at by German aircraft.

About 340,000 French, Belgians, and British troops were rescued from Dunkirk.

Dunkirk evacuation
British and French troops, cut off by the rapid German advance, had either to escape by sea to Britain or surrender. They held on to Dunkirk, on France's Channel coast, for nine days. During that time Royal Navy warships evacuated thousands of troops through Dunkirk port, and hundreds of small boats also pitched in and ferried soldiers from beaches to larger ships off shore.

Perilous escape
Allied troops at Dunkirk were under constant *Luftwaffe* bombing, and many ships were sunk. Soldiers waded out to sea to be rescued. Many of the soldiers who reached Britain were shocked by their experience.

"The Royal Navy, with the willing help of countless merchant seamen, strained every nerve to embark the British and Allied troops."

Winston Churchill to the House of Commons, June 4, 1940

A total of 338,000 Allied troops were evacuated from Dunkirk by the Royal Navy between May 27–June 4, 1940

BRITAIN STANDS ALONE

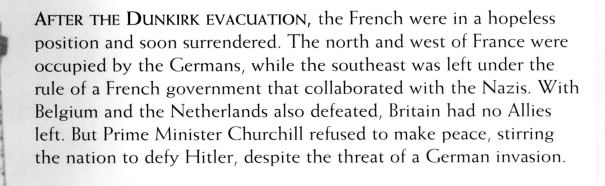

AFTER THE DUNKIRK EVACUATION, the French were in a hopeless position and soon surrendered. The north and west of France were occupied by the Germans, while the southeast was left under the rule of a French government that collaborated with the Nazis. With Belgium and the Netherlands also defeated, Britain had no Allies left. But Prime Minister Churchill refused to make peace, stirring the nation to defy Hitler, despite the threat of a German invasion.

Hitler triumphant

Defeating France in just six weeks was an extraordinary achievement for Hitler, giving him sweet revenge for the defeat of Germany in World War I. He forced the French to sign an armistice in exactly the same place where Germany had surrendered in 1918.
Then, on June 28, 1940, Hitler spent a day sightseeing in Paris, the French capital.

Pétain leads Vichy France

After the French surrender, Marshal Philippe Pétain ruled one-third of France from the spa town of Vichy. Pétain was 84 years old and was a war hero of World War I. His government's slogan was "Work, Family, and the Fatherland." Vichy France collaborated with the Germans, abolished democracy, and discriminated against Jews.

De Gaulle heads Free French

French army officer General Charles de Gaulle set up a Free French movement in London. He wanted the French to keep up the fight against Germany. De Gaulle won support from those opposed to the Vichy government.

Churchill speaks for Britain

The British government included members of all political parties. After France fell, there were calls to make peace with Germany, but most people supported Churchill in rejecting any deal with Hitler. The prime minister rallied national morale with stirring speeches broadcast on the radio. He said that he had "nothing to offer but blood, toil, tears, and sweat."

Sinking of French fleet

Churchill feared that the French Navy would fall into German hands. At Mers-el-Kebir in Algeria, the Royal Navy fired on and sank French warships in port. More than 1,200 French sailors were killed in five minutes of shelling. This greatly angered many people in France.

Home Guard

In the summer os 1940, Britain prepared to face a German invasion. Beaches were blocked with mines and barbed wire, and small concrete forts (pill boxes) were built. More than a million men, many of them too old to serve in the army, joined the part-time Home Guard. Nicknamed "Dad's Army," they were poorly armed but were positioned to look out for German paratroopers and spies.

In his radio broadcasts, Churchill inspired the British population, declaring "Hitler knows that he will have to break us in this island, or lose the war."

Imprisoned aliens

The fear of enemy agents led to thousands of foreigners living in Britain being imprisoned in camps, notably on the Isle of Man. Many of the "enemy aliens"—mostly from Germany, Austria, and Italy—were opposed to Nazism and Fascism. Eventually released, many "aliens" contributed to the British war effort.

BATTLE OF BRITAIN AND THE BLITZ

WITH FRANCE DEFEATED, Germany based its aircraft along the French Channel coast, within a few minutes' flying time of England. The *Luftwaffe* set out to destroy the Royal Air Force (RAF), while the German army prepared to invade Britain by sea. However, Germany called off the invasion, so the Battle of Britain was fought solely in the air. Unable to crush the RAF, the *Luftwaffe* bombed Britain's cities by night—a campaign known as The Blitz.

RAF on the defensive
In the summer of 1940, daytime air battles took place over southern England. RAF fighter pilots in Spitfires and Hurricanes took on *Luftwaffe* bombers with *Messerschmitt* fighters as escorts. When a German aircraft was spotted, RAF pilots were ordered to "scramble"– run to their aircraft—since every second saved was vital.

RADAR EARLY WARNING

Britain had developed a sophisticated system of air defense. Radar stations on the coast spotted German aircraft approaching. They relayed the information to command centers, where the movements of the enemy aircraft were plotted by pushing blocks around on a large map table. The RAF airfields were then contacted and fighter squadrons were told where to fly to meet the advancing intruders.

Battle of Britain Day
On September 15, 1940, now celebrated as Battle of Britain Day, more than 1,000 German aircraft attacked the RAF. The British pilots were outnumbered, but the *Luftwaffe* lost 60 aircraft, while the RAF lost 28. It was clear that the RAF could not be defeated. Churchill praised the British pilots, saying, "Never in the field of human conflict was so much owed by so many to so few."

Bombers over London

The first major bombing raid on London was on September 7, 1940. Bombers attacked by night, as well as by day, when the RAF had less chance of shooting them down. By May 10, 1941, around 43,000 people had been killed by bombing in Britain's cities.

London Burning

The Blitz put a huge strain on the emergency services. The *Luftwaffe* dropped incendiary bombs—designed to start fires—as well as explosive bombs that flattened buildings. In London there were sometimes more than 2,000 fires on a single night. The light from blazing buildings guided more bombers to their target.

Sheltering in the Underground

Thousands of people escaped the bombs by sleeping on the platforms of Underground stations. The stations were very smelly, overcrowded, and uncomfortable, but they made people feel safe. Later, conditions were improved, with bunks installed for sleeping.

Coventry destroyed

Many cities were bombed duri The Blitz, including Liverpool Glasgow, Plymouth, and Belfas but none was hit worse than Coventry. On the night of November 14–15, 1940, a flee of *Luftwaffe* bombers devastatec the city center. The buildings destroyed included the city's medieval cathedral. More than 500 people died in one night.

VOICES
THE BLITZ

During the bombing of Britain's cities by the *Luftwaffe* from September 1940 to May 1941, civilians took cover as best they could—under the stairs, in flimsy Anderson shelters in their yards, in public shelters, or in London Underground stations. The "Blitz spirit" drew people together in their shared fear and suffering.

"*THOSE OF US who were left in London became quite used to the routine of early evening. For a while we sheltered in our own Anderson shelter, but then we found that everyone was 'going down the tube.' The children in siren-suits and mother carrying whatever she thought we might need: food, blankets, comics—anything in fact. There was no rush, no panic, just a steady stream of people making for the shelter... The tube trains still ran, of course, and they still had to cope with passengers, and I remember we had to sleep on the platforms and there was a white painted line beyond which we were not allowed to lie. After the last train, of course, it got much better... We were encouraged to sing in the shelters... How they found the enthusiasm for this I don't know...*"

Six-year-old Elizabeth Le Blond was one of the few among her friends not evacuated from London.

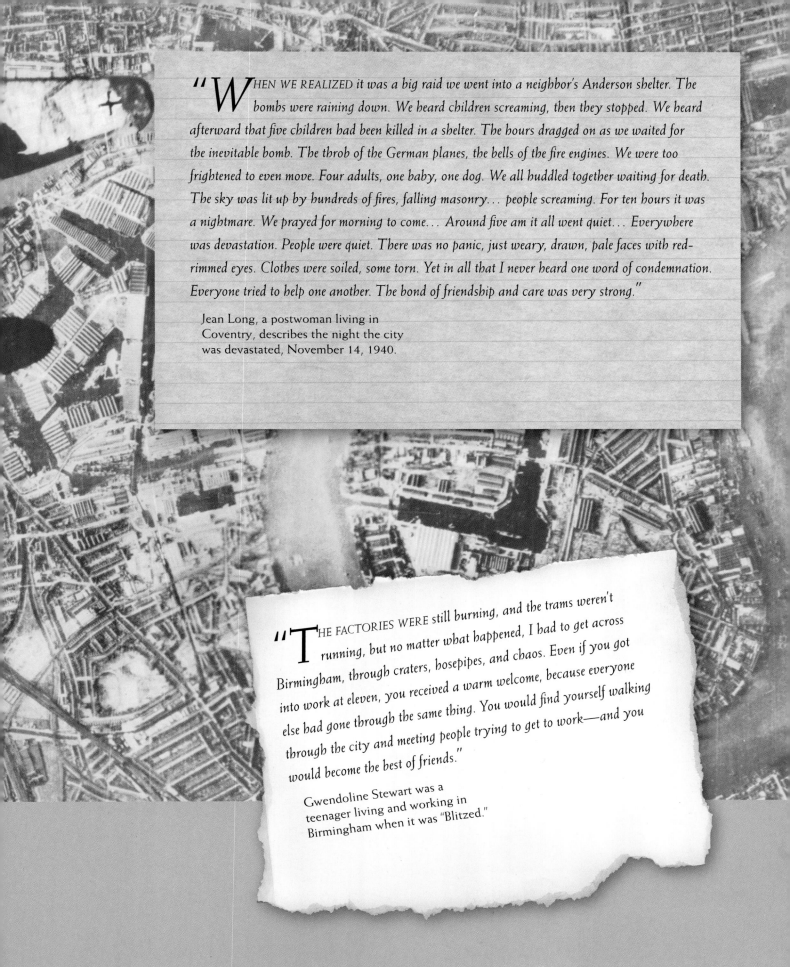

"WHEN WE REALIZED it was a big raid we went into a neighbor's Anderson shelter. The bombs were raining down. We heard children screaming, then they stopped. We heard afterward that five children had been killed in a shelter. The hours dragged on as we waited for the inevitable bomb. The throb of the German planes, the bells of the fire engines. We were too frightened to even move. Four adults, one baby, one dog. We all huddled together waiting for death. The sky was lit up by hundreds of fires, falling masonry... people screaming. For ten hours it was a nightmare. We prayed for morning to come... Around five am it all went quiet... Everywhere was devastation. People were quiet. There was no panic, just weary, drawn, pale faces with red-rimmed eyes. Clothes were soiled, some torn. Yet in all that I never heard one word of condemnation. Everyone tried to help one another. The bond of friendship and care was very strong."

Jean Long, a postwoman living in
Coventry, describes the night the city
was devastated, November 14, 1940.

"THE FACTORIES WERE still burning, and the trams weren't running, but no matter what happened, I had to get across Birmingham, through craters, hosepipes, and chaos. Even if you got into work at eleven, you received a warm welcome, because everyone else had gone through the same thing. You would find yourself walking through the city and meeting people trying to get to work—and you would become the best of friends."

Gwendoline Stewart was a
teenager living and working in
Birmingham when it was "Blitzed."

AMERICA BACKS BRITAIN

BY 1941 IT WAS CLEAR THAT, for the time being, Germany had failed to defeat Britain. But the British were in a desperate state and could not have continued fighting without the help of American money and goods. US President Roosevelt was convinced that a victory for Hitler would be a disaster for the United States, but the American people were against getting involved in a foreign war. Roosevelt inched toward outright support for Britain, telling Americans that the US must be the "arsenal of democracy"—providing the weapons for the British to fight Hitler.

Americans prosper
Life was looking up for Americans in 1940–41. As US industry began producing large quantities of war equipment—not only to arm Britain, but also to expand its own armed forces—jobs were plentiful and wages rose. Americans with money in their pockets felt they had better things to do than fight a war. Joe DiMaggio's skills on the baseball field interested them much more than foreign politics.

America First
The famous American airman Charles Lindbergh was one of the most prominent spokesmen for the America First movement, which campaigned to keep the United States out of involvement in the European war. Opinion polls showed that only one in five Americans was prepared to join the fight against Hitler. In 1940, when Roosevelt stood for reelection as president, he had to promise the United States would only go to war if attacked.

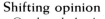

Shifting opinion
On the whole, Americans wanted Britain to succeed in its war against the Nazis. They admired the way the British stood up to bombing in The Blitz, and disliked Hitler's bullying militarism and police state. *The Great Dictator*, a movie in which comic actor Charlie Chaplin played the power-crazed Adenoid Hynkel—an obvious satire on Adolf Hitler—was a popular hit in American movie theaters in 1940.

From Cash-and-Carry to Lend-lease
From the start of the war, the US supplied the British with arms and other goods as long as they could pay for and transport them. In 1940 Roosevelt also agreed to give the Royal Navy 50 old destroyers in return for a lease on some British bases. From the spring of 1941, the Lend-lease program allowed Britain to "borrow" goods from the United States without payment.

Fragile lifeline

Goods from the United States had to be carried across the Atlantic by ship. Britain's ocean lifeline was threatened by German U-boats, which, from the summer of 1940, had bases in France. The US Navy became increasingly involved in protecting Atlantic convoys as U-boats sank American merchant ships.

Atlantic Charter

In August 1941, Churchill and Roosevelt met on a warship off Newfoundland in Canada. They agreed on a statement of war goals, known as the Atlantic Charter. They wanted to create a world in which, after the defeat of the Nazis, people could live "in freedom from want and fear." At this point, the US was clearly committed to the war against Hitler in every way short of actual fighting.

IMPERIAL SUPPORT

Britain never really "stood alone" because it always had the support of its dominions and colonies. Canada backed Britain's war effort by generously providing both men and money. Australians, New Zealanders, and South Africans fought, especially in North Africa. West Indians and people from African colonies served in British forces and were recruited as skilled workers. India's army had the most men, 2.5 million in total, all of them volunteers.

THE BRITISH COMMONWEALTH OF NATIONS

TOGETHER

ITALY GOES TO WAR

DESPITE HIS "PACT OF STEEL" with Nazi Germany, Italian Fascist dictator Benito Mussolini at first kept out of the war. He knew that his armed forces were not prepared to fight against a major power, such as Britain or France. It was not until the Allies looked beaten in June 1940 that Mussolini hastily joined in on the "winning side." But things went badly for the Italians, who soon faced defeat in Africa and Greece.

Italy takes advantage
Mussolini declared war on France and Britain on June 10, 1940. This poster shows Mussolini and Hitler sowing the fields of Europe with tanks and guns, and represents the Italian leader's desire for his country to reap the harvest of a certain German victory. Italian troops invaded southern France, but performed poorly in two weeks' fighting.

Sinkings at Taranto
Mussolini bragged that the Mediterranean was *Mare Nostrum*—Latin for "Our Sea." But Britain's Royal Navy soon gave the Italian fleet a scare. In November 1940, Swordfish aircraft launched from the carrier *Illustrious* attacked the Italian naval base at Taranto, sinking three battleships with torpedoes.

Emperor returns
In the spring of 1941, British forces, made up of mostly Indian and African troops, defeated the Italians in their East African colonies—Eritrea, Italian Somaliland, and Ethiopia. The Ethiopian Emperor Haile Selassie returned to his homeland exactly five years after being driven out by Mussolini's forces in May 1936.

Desert Rats

Italy's entry into the war brought fighting to the North African desert. The Italians used their colony, Libya, as a base for invading Egypt, where British troops were stationed. This threatened the vital waterway of the Suez Canal. The British 7th Armoured Division—the "Desert Rats"—and an Australian division counterattacked, driving the Italians out of Egypt and advancing into Libya.

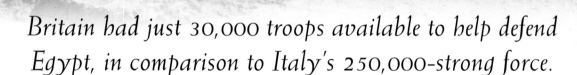

Britain had just 30,000 troops available to help defend Egypt, in comparison to Italy's 250,000-strong force.

Italian surrender

The Italian forces in North Africa greatly outnumbered British and Commonwealth forces, but they were badly led and poorly equipped. In 10 weeks' fighting they were driven back 500 miles (800 km) across Libya. Around 130,000 Italians surrendered and were marched off to prisoner-of-war camps. The success of the desert campaign heartened Britain at a time when the rest of the war was going badly.

British troops sent to Greece

Italy also attacked Greece, invading from Albania. Once again, Italian troops performed badly. In the spring of 1941, British and Australian troops were sent from North Africa to Greece. This proved to be an unwise move because it stopped Britain from completing its victory over the Italians in North Africa, while in the end it failed to help the Greeks.

GERMANS ENTER THE MEDITERRANEAN

HITLER WAS FORCED TO INTERVENE in the fighting in the Mediterranean because of the embarrassing failures of his ally Mussolini. In another stunning series of *Blitzkrieg* lightning victories, the Germans conquered Yugoslavia, drove the British out of Greece, and then seized the island of Crete with a bold airborne attack. Meanwhile, the tanks of the German Afrika Korps under the command of Erwin Rommel rolled into North Africa.

Rommel arrives

German tank commander Rommel, who had played a leading role in the defeat of France, arrived in North Africa in February 1941. His Afrika Korps proved far better than the British at tank warfare in the desert. Nicknamed the "Desert Fox," Rommel was admired by ally and enemy alike for his military skills, his dash, and daring.

The Desert War, March 1941 to July 1942

The tide of battle swept backward and forward along the coastal strip of northern Libya and Egypt. In spring 1941, Rommel drove the British back to the Egyptian border. The British then counterattacked, but in the summer of 1942 the Afrika Korps advanced as far as El Alamein, deep inside Egypt.

The Desert War

Area of fighting

Fighting in the desert

Heat, flies, and dust all made the desert a difficult place to fight. But it was ideal tank country, with few obstacles aside from the sand dunes. It was also largely uninhabited, so civilian casualties were minimal. Armies used minefields and antitank guns to block the advance of enemy tanks.

Invasion of Yugoslavia and Greece

☐ Germany and allies
→ German advance

From the Balkans to Crete
In April 1941, the Germans invaded Yugoslavia, which fell in 12 days. The Germans then rapidly overran Greece and seized Crete. The whole campaign took less than two months.

Airborne invasion
German paratroopers were dropped into Crete on May 20, 1941. Although many were killed by British Commonwealth troops, they succeeded in capturing an airfield, allowing German aircraft to land more soldiers and equipment. The Royal Navy evacuated thousands of troops from Crete to Egypt. Those left behind surrendered.

In March and April 1942, 8,800 tons of bombs were dropped on Malta, twice the amount that was dropped on London during The Blitz.

Malta struggles to survive
From 1940 to 1942, the British-ruled island of Malta was bombed by Italian aircraft and the German *Luftwaffe* based in nearby Sicily. Ships heading for the island were also savaged. The Maltese people held out despite near starvation, and the island was awarded the British George Cross for bravery.

BARBAROSSA

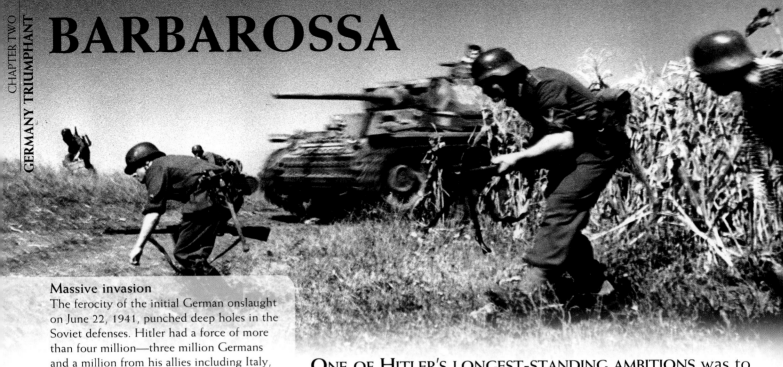

Massive invasion

The ferocity of the initial German onslaught on June 22, 1941, punched deep holes in the Soviet defenses. Hitler had a force of more than four million—three million Germans and a million from his allies including Italy, Romania, Hungary, Slovakia, and Finland.

Operation Barbarossa, 1941

→	German advance
—	German borders, June 21
– – –	German front line, September 1
–·–·–	German front line, November 15
········	German front line, December 5
– · · –	Pocket of Soviet troops

FINLAND

0 km 100 200 300
0 miles 100 200

Leningrad

Gulf of Finland Narva
Tallinn

Estonia

Novgorod

Latvia
Riga

Kalinin

Moscow

Memel
Dvinsk
Lithuania
Kaunas

Vyaz'ma
Tula
Smolensk

Minsk
Bryansk
Orel

SOVIET UNION

Kursk

Bialystok

Belgorod

Brest-Litovsk
Khar'kov

Kiev

Nazi-occupied
Poland

Ukraine

Tarnopol
Umam'
Rostov

SLOVAKIA

HUNGARY

Kherson
Sea of Azov
Odessa
Kerch

ROMANIA

Sevastopol
Black Sea

ONE OF HITLER'S LONGEST-STANDING AMBITIONS was to conquer the Soviet Union. In June 1941, the Germans and their allies swarmed across the Soviet border in Operation Barbarossa. At first the German invasion seemed an overwhelming success, with the Soviets suffering massive losses. However, a combination of severe winter weather and determined Soviet counterattacks eventually brought the German advance to a halt. Hitler did not get the quick victory that he needed.

Barbarossa, June–December 1941

Moving rapidly in their usual *Blitzkrieg* style, the Germans outflanked and surrounded Soviet armies, forcing hundreds of thousands of soldiers to surrender. But the invaders failed to take Leningrad (St. Petersburg) or Moscow, the two major Soviet cities.

Warm welcome

In Ukraine and the Baltic States, German troops were at first welcomed by local people as liberators from the rule of Soviet dictator, Stalin. This German accepts bread from grateful Ukrainians, but the Nazis' brutality soon made enemies of those who had greeted them.

Soviet resistance

After initial disasters, the Russian people rallied to the desperate defense of their homeland, spurred on by patriotic posters such as this. German tanks advanced to within 20 miles (32 km) of Moscow, but a decisive Soviet counterattack in December 1941, commanded by General Georgi Zhukov, drove them back.

Winter weather

Expecting a quick victory, the Germans had not equipped themselves for the extreme cold of the Russian winter. Soldiers suffered cruely, some losing feet and fingers through frostbite, while equipment failed to work for lack of heaters and antifreeze.

Heavy casualties

The savagery of the fighting in the Soviet Union was awesome. The Germans lost around 750,000 men, killed or wounded in the first six months. Soviet losses were far higher—about 3.5 million dead and 3.5 million taken prisoner—but the Soviet Union had a large enough population to replace the men lost.

Strange allies

Although British Prime Minister Churchill hated communism, he welcomed Stalin as an ally against Hitler. Britain, soon joined by the United States, began supplying the Soviets with equipment. In September 1941, the British government declared a "Tanks for Russia" week to publicize arms production for the Soviet Union.

"The war against Russia
will be such that it cannot
be conducted in a knightly
fashion. This struggle is one of
ideologies and racial differences
and will have to be conducted
with unprecedented, unmerciful,
and unrelenting harshness."

Adolf Hitler, March 1941

A farm is set ablaze by German soldiers as they advance into the Soviet Union in 1941

MASSACRE AND STARVATION

Jews massacred
Special SS (Nazi security organization) execution squads called *Einsatzgruppen* ("task forces") accompanied the German army into the Soviet Union, killing hundreds of thousands of Jewish people. Jews were often shot and buried in mass graves. Almost 34,000 were killed in a few days at Babi Yar, outside Kiev.

THE GERMAN INVASION OF THE SOVIET UNION brought terrible suffering. German troops had orders to behave with total ruthlessness, and massacres occurred wherever they advanced. Hitler cared nothing for Russian people, whom he despised as Slavs—in his view an inferior race—and as communists. There were also many Jews in the Soviet Union, whom the Nazis sought to exterminate. Stalin was merciless toward his own people, using terror to keep them under control. In a war between two brutal dictatorships, ordinary people had nowhere to hide.

Slavs targeted
Hitler intended for German people to live in Russia and Ukraine, so he was happy to see large numbers of Slavs die as well as Jews. SS chief Heinrich Himmler estimated that up to 30 million Soviet citizens needed to be eliminated by starvation or massacre. The Germans destroyed buildings and killed civilians on the slightest pretext.

Partisans
In German-occupied areas, Soviet civilians formed partisan—armed resistance—groups, carrying out ambushes, sabotage, and raids against the Germans. Any partisans who were caught were executed, as was anyone suspected of aiding them. The German army had orders to kill 50 to 100 Soviet citizens for every soldier killed by partisans.

Leningrad starves

German and Finnish forces surrounded
Leningrad (St. Petersburg) in 1941. Food soon
ran out, and the people trapped inside the city
began to starve. They were also bombarded by
aircraft and artillery. In winter, the Soviets
managed to send in some supplies across a
frozen lake, but the siege lasted for 900 days,
during which time about a million people died.

Russian prisoners of war

Soviet soldiers taken prisoner by the
Germans stood little chance of survival.
Some were executed, many more
died of neglect and starvation in
German camps. Out of more
than 5 million prisoners in
total, at least 3.5 million
died in captivity.

Fighting Stalinist oppression

About one million Soviets fought alongside Germany. Many were
from national minorities, including Latvians, Lithuanians,
Estonians, Ukrainians, and Chechens. They had suffered under
Stalin's rule and wanted to fight back. Stalin took brutal revenge
on traitors, and in 1944 deported the entire Chechen people to a
remote wasteland, condemning at least 230,000 of them to death.

WAR IN THE PACIFIC

WHEN JAPAN ATTACKED the US naval base at Pearl Harbor on December 7, 1941, it brought the United States into World War II, which at last became a truly worldwide conflict. Early successes gave the Japanese control of much of the Pacific and Southeast Asia, but the US soon began to hit back. The war in the Pacific and Asia developed into a conflict fought primarily by aircraft carriers at sea, and by infantry in jungles and on Pacific islands.

Guadalcanal marines
American troops arrive at Guadalcanal island
to begin the first Allied offensive in the Pacific.

July 21
Japanese troops occupy French Indochina; the US and Britain impose economic sanctions

December 10
The British warships *Prince of Wales* and *Repulse* are sunk by Japanese aircraft

January
Admiral Isoroku Yamamoto begins preparations for a Japanese raid on Pearl Harbor

December 7
Japanese naval aircraft, launched from carriers, attack the American base at Pearl Harbor, Hawaii, bringing the US into the war

1941

April 13
Japan and the Soviet Union sign a neutrality pact

December 8
Japanese forces invade the Philippines and Malaya, and occupy Hong Kong

December 25
Hong Kong falls to the Japanese

October 16
General Hideki Tojo becomes prime minister of Japan

December 11
Germany and Italy declare war on the US

April 18
US aircraft bomb
Tokyo in the
Doolittle raid

May 31
By the end of May, Japanese troops
complete the conquest of the Dutch
East Indies, the Philippines, and Burma

February 15
The garrison of the
British base at Singapore
surrenders to the Japanese

May 8
US and Japanese aircraft
carriers duel at the Battle
of the Coral Sea

July 14
Indian nationalists, led by Gandhi,
launch the "Quit India" movement
against British rule in India

1942

April 9
The Bataan peninsula
in the Philippines falls
to the Japanese

June 7
The US Navy wins the Battle of
Midway after three days' fighting,
sinking four Japanese aircraft carriers

August 8
US troops capture the airstrip at
Henderson Field on Guadalcanal,
one of the Solomon Islands

February 19
Japan carries out air raids on
the Australian city of Darwin

July 12
Fighting begins between
Australian and Japanese
troops in New Guinea

Asia and the Pacific in 1940

■ British possessions
■ French possessions
□ Japan and Japanese possessions
□ Netherlands possessions
■ United States and United States possessions

SOVIET UNION

CANADA

MONGOLIA   Manchukuo

UNITED STATES

CHINA   KOREA

JAPAN   PACIFIC OCEAN

TIBET

NEPAL   BHUTAN

INDIA   Macao (Portugal)   Hong Kong (UK)

BURMA

Taiwan (Japan)

Mariana Islands (Japan)

Hawaiian Islands (US)

SIAM   FRENCH INDO-CHINA   PHILIPPINES

Guam (US)

Marshall Islands (Japan)

BRITISH NORTH BORNEO   BRUNEI   SARAWAK

Caroline Islands (Japan)

MALAYA

Singapore (UK)

DUTCH EAST INDIES

INDIAN OCEAN

Solomon Islands (UK)

PORTUGUESE TIMOR

0 km 1000 2000 3000
0 miles 1000 2000

Asia and the Pacific in 1940

The Netherlands, France, and Britain all had colonies in Asia, and the US controlled the Philippines. Japan wanted to take over the Dutch East Indies (Indonesia), and already occupied much of China, Korea, and Formosa (Taiwan).

Powerful fleet

Japan had the most powerful navy in the Pacific. In 1940, feeling menaced by both Japan and Germany, the US decided to expand its navy until it was capable of fighting wars in the Atlantic and the Pacific at the same time. Japanese leaders knew that they might be able to defeat the Americans at sea if they struck before this shipbuilding program really got under way.

THE UNITED STATES CONFRONTS JAPAN

AFTER INVADING CHINA in 1937, the Japanese moved troops into French Indochina (Vietnam) in 1940–41. The US demanded that Japan withdraw its forces from China and Indochina in summer 1941. The Japanese refused. The United States responded by blockading essential supplies to Japan. This left the Japanese with the choice of giving up their ambition to conquer an Asian empire, or going to war with the US. They chose war.

平太下天助協満華日

Co-Prosperity Sphere

In August 1940, Japan announced its intention to group Asian countries into a "Co-Prosperity Sphere." In reality, this meant Japan intended to conquer the rest of Asia. This Japanese propaganda poster hails the supposed friendship between peace-loving Japan, China, and Manchukuo (the Japanese name for the puppet state of Manchuria).

AXIS PARTNER

In September 1940, Japan signed a formal Axis alliance with Nazi Germany and Fascist Italy. Germany's ongoing war with Britain, and the German defeat of France and the Netherlands, gave Japan the opportunity to attack the European empires in Asia. But by joining the Axis powers, Japan raised American fears. US President Roosevelt believed that the three Axis powers planned to "unite in ultimate action against the United States."

US support for China

By 1941 the US was supplying a lot of military aid to Chiang Kai-shek's Chinese Nationalist government to help it fight the Japanese. US pilots and technicians formed a volunteer group known as the Flying Tigers to help the Chinese resist Japanese air power. The US airmen were in China by late 1941.

Tojo becomes prime minister

Military leaders controlled the Japanese government. General Hideki Tojo, the former army chief of staff, became prime minister in October 1941. Tojo planned to attack the European colonies in Asia, and the United States in the Pacific.

Strength and weakness

The Japanese were intensely patriotic, and their armed forces were large. Japanese soldiers were trained to fight to the death for their emperor. But Japan was a much smaller, poorer country than the US. Its leaders had to hope that fighting spirit and swift military victories would allow their country to triumph, despite its weaknesses.

PEARL HARBOR

ON DECEMBER 7, 1941, Japanese aircraft attacked the American fleet at Pearl Harbor in Hawaii. Coming before Japan had declared war, the air strikes were a total surprise. Eighteen warships were sunk or damaged, and nearly 200 aircraft destroyed. The Pearl Harbor mission was a huge success for the Japanese, but the "sneak" attack made Americans determined to have revenge.

Admiral Yamamoto
The man behind the attack on Pearl Harbor was Admiral Isoroku Yamamoto. He had opposed a war between Japan and the US because he felt that in the long run Japan would lose. But if a war had to be fought, he believed Japan had to destroy the US Pacific fleet right at the start.

Naval fliers
Japan's carrier aircraft, such as the Zero fighter, were the best in the world. The highly trained pilots had effective bombs and torpedoes. Admiral Yamamoto naturally turned to his naval fliers to deliver a knockout blow against the US Navy.

Almost 2,400 Americans were killed at Pearl Harbor; only 64 Japanese died.

Secret attack
Six Japanese carriers, with 400 aircraft, secretly left Japan on November 26 and headed for Hawaii. The carriers got to within 250 miles (400 km) of Pearl Harbor before launching their aircraft.

Devastating strike

The first wave of 185 Japanese aircraft struck Pearl Harbor at 7:48 a.m. It was a Sunday, and American forces were following a rest-day routine. Many men were still in bed when the first bombs hit warships in the harbor. Zero fighters shot up US aircraft before they could get off the ground. A second wave soon followed.

Heroic resistance

American servicemen struggled to organize antiaircraft fire. One hero on the day was African-American ship's cook Dorie Miller, who was decorated for operating a machine gun to shoot down Japanese planes.

Battleship losses

The Japanese attack caused mayhem in the crowded port. The three largest US warships were sunk. The worst casualty was the USS *Arizona*, which exploded, killing almost a thousand men. Luckily for the Americans, their three aircraft carriers were away from port and so survived.

"Remember Pearl Harbor"

The memory of Pearl Harbor was used to rally American people to fight harder to defeat Japan. Most Americans hated the Japanese far more than they did their German or Italian enemies.

...we here highly resolve that these dead shall not have died in vain...

REMEMBER DEC. 7th!

The battleships USS *West Virginia* (foreground) and *Tennessee* burn after the Japanese surprise attack on Pearl Harbor. However, neither of these ships sank

"I ask that the Congress declare that since the unprovoked and dastardly attack by Japan on Sunday, December 7, 1941, a state of war has existed between the United States and the Japanese Empire."

President Roosevelt's speech to Congress, calling for a declaration of war, December 8, 1941

THE UNITED STATES GOES TO WAR

OUTRAGE AT THE ATTACK on Pearl Harbor united Americans in favor of going to war. The United States went almost immediately to war with Germany and Italy, as well as Japan. Americans may have been eager to fight, but they were not necessarily well prepared, despite the beginnings of a military buildup in 1940–41. As a result, the United States had to transform millions of civilians into soldiers and turn its industrial might to war production on a vast scale.

Day of infamy
The day after the Pearl Harbor attack, American President Roosevelt addressed the US Congress. He said that December 7, 1941, was a "date which will live in infamy" and declared the start of a long-term struggle for victory over Japan.

Hitler declares war
Adolf Hitler saved the US government a lot of trouble by declaring war on the US in support of Japan. Italy followed suit. Had this not happened, US public opinion might have forced the president to stay at peace with Germany and Italy, to concentrate on fighting Japan.

Europe first

America's entry into the war was a great relief to Britain. Late in December 1941, Roosevelt met with British Prime Minister Churchill in Washington, D.C., (the Arcadia Conference). They adopted a "Europe First" policy that gave priority to defeating Germany, relegating the war against Japan to second place.

Japanese imprisoned

Thousands of Japanese-Americans living on the west coast of the United States were interned in camps. This unjust policy showed the depth of feeling against the Japanese. Americans of German or Italian origin were not imprisoned. Some Japanese-Americans were later allowed to fight for the US army in segregated units.

SEGREGATED ARMY

This image of boxer Joe Louis was used to gain African-American support for the war. But the US army was racially segregated, with black soldiers serving in separate units from whites. As the war went on, growing numbers of African-Americans proved their worth as fighting men.

Pvt. Joe Louis says...

"We're going to do our part ... and we'll win because we're on God's side"

Conscripting GIs

First introduced in the US in 1940, conscription built up the US Army into an impressive force. Many Americans who had been unemployed since the Depression welcomed the security and good food they got as GIs ("Government Issue," or ordinary soldiers). But training and equipping troops took time. Few US soldiers did any fighting until the country had been at war for almost a year.

Doolittle raid

In April 1942, US bombers, led by Lieutenant Colonel Jimmy Doolittle, flew from an aircraft carrier to bomb Tokyo, Japan, which was far out of range of land-based bombers. This token gesture served to boost American morale.

JAPAN'S LIGHTNING VICTORIES

THE INITIAL SUCCESSES OF THE JAPANESE were spectacular. In six months they had conquered the Philippines, Malaya, Singapore, the Dutch East Indies, and Burma, and invaded New Guinea. Japanese soldiers moved fast and fought with fierce commitment, backed up by naval and air power. Their rapid progress brought them to the border of British-ruled India, and threatened Australia with invasion.

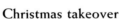

Christmas takeover
Japanese troops attacked the British colony of Hong Kong from southern China. After mounting a brave defense, the British, Indians, and Canadians surrendered their base on Christmas Day 1941. Japanese occupation brought years of hardship to the city. Almost a million people fled to China in search of food.

Warships sunk
On December 10, 1941, two British warships, *Prince of Wales* and *Repulse*, were sunk as they tried to stop Japan from invading Malaya. More than 800 sailors died, although almost 1,300 were rescued. The British did not have the resources to fight against Japan and Germany.

Fast-moving army
The Japanese moved through difficult jungle terrain at a speed that amazed their enemies. Living off light rations, their soldiers made only limited use of trucks or armored vehicles, often traveling on bicycles.

Defending Australia

There were real fears of a Japanese invasion of Australia. In February 1942, Darwin, a city in Australia's Northern Territory, was heavily bombed by Japanese aircraft. Other raids followed. Australian troops were called back from the Middle East to build barricades around Darwin.

Singapore is lost

Attacked by Japanese soldiers who had overrun Malaya, the British base at Singapore fell in February 1942. The sight of British officers surrendering to the Japanese was a shock in a world used to the idea that white people were racially superior to Asians. The British Empire's reputation never recovered.

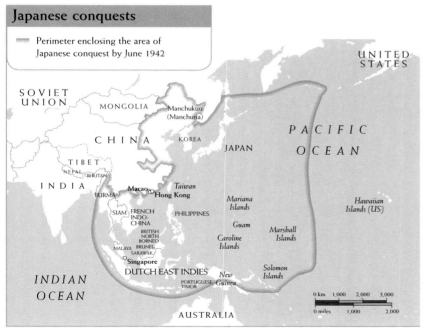

American surrender

Filipino and American troops on the Philippines, led by General Douglas MacArthur, fought a lengthy defensive action against Japanese forces. Most of MacArthur's army surrendered in April 1942—the only US army ever to concede defeat to a foreign enemy. MacArthur had left the Philippines shortly before, vowing to return.

Japanese conquests

Perimeter enclosing the area of Japanese conquest by June 1942

By June 1942, conquests had given Japan all the raw materials it needed to continue the war. Most important were oil from the Dutch East Indies and rubber from Malaya. Japan wanted to maintain a defensive perimeter against the United States.

69

PRISONERS OF THE JAPANESE

TENS OF THOUSANDS OF ALLIED SOLDIERS and civilians fell into Japanese hands. Japanese soldiers had been taught that surrender was shameful and felt contempt for men who had allowed themselves to become prisoners of war (PoWs). Prisoners were subjected to neglect and deliberate cruelty.

Bataan death march
After their surrender in the Philippines in April 1942, American and Filipino troops on the Bataan peninsula were forced to march a long way without food or water, and were beaten by guards. Some 15,000 died on the march, about one in five of those who set out.

Approximately one in three of all Allied soldiers who were taken prisoner by the Japanese died in captivity.

Changi camp
One of the largest Japanese PoW camps was at Changi in Singapore. Many of these British and Australian prisoners never even got a chance to fight. They arrived in Singapore shortly before it was captured and were bitter at having surrendered without a fight.

Selarang incident

The Japanese were ruthless in imposing their own rules on prisoners who tried to uphold what they regarded as the rules of war. In one incident at Changi in 1942, the Japanese wanted prisoners to sign a paper promising not to escape. When they refused, 16,000 men were herded into Selarang Barracks (right) and left to starve. The prisoners saved their lives by eventually signing as ordered.

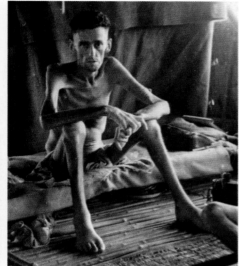

Inadequate rations

Although punishments and beatings did cause deaths, the main threats to prisoners' survival were disease and malnutrition. Prisoners tried to grow their own food to add to their small daily rice ration. If lack of food made a man too weak to work, the Japanese might stop his rations altogether.

Women and children prisoners

Civilian women and children also fell into Japanese hands, and were interned in camps where conditions were often as bad as those for Allied troops. This picture, painted by war artist Leslie Cole, shows British women and children in the camp at Syme Road, Singapore.

Railroad of death

In June 1942 the Japanese began constructing a railroad from Thailand to Burma. About 200,000 Asian laborers and 60,000 PoWs—mostly British, Australian, and Dutch—were forced to work on this "Death Railroad." More than a quarter of the prisoners, and half of the Asians, died from disease, maltreatment, and overwork. When the railroad was completed in October 1943, most of the surviving PoWs were shipped to work in Japan.

VOICES
JAPANESE POWS

Allied soldiers captured by the Japanese suffered terribly from lack of food, overwork, and general mistreatment. Punishments were brutal in the extreme. To survive, a prisoner needed a great will to live and considerable good luck.

"A JAPANESE SERGEANT-MAJOR got us all on parade, arranged on three sides of a square, so that nobody could miss what was going to happen. Eventually, these poor creatures were led out, hands tied behind their backs, staggering as the Japanese prodded them. One was placed opposite each grave... Then the Japanese officer signaled and three young Japanese soldiers left the ranks. One stood opposite each prisoner with a fixed bayonet... The Japanese officer made his men practice bayonet drill on these men... They threw the men still kicking into the graves."

British Flight Sergeant David Russell was in a Japanese prison camp on Java.

"GOD! HOW DAMN cold this last night was! If God wills may this next one be warmer, for the benefit of all... In the hospital area this morning we received one light cup of rice per man and about one half-cup of bilge water. Terrible water; I don't see how it will sustain us. Dr. Lambert died this morning from diarrhea, the cold, the lack of food and water. Many are dying every night now. My left foot is gradually getting worse and there remains nothing to do but pray and wait."

Cecil J. Peart was a US Marine pharmacist.

*"I*N THE CAMP *we lived in huts made of bamboo, which we had to build ourselves. Just a bamboo platform 18 inches off the ground and a palm-leafed roof over the top. No sides, so the mosquitoes had a whale of a time. No blankets except what you owned yourself. No clothes or food utensils were issued. So it was a pint of rice in the morning, then we marched out of the camp and onto the railway before dawn. At midday they would let us stop for some more rice, then we carried on working until it was dark and we were marched back to the camp... If it poured with rain you carried on working, boiling sunshine or monsoon, you just carried on. We liked the monsoon because we had a bath."*

British Marine Peter Dunstan was forced
to work on the Burma-Thailand railroad.

CARRIER BATTLES

UNTIL WORLD WAR II, naval battles had been fought by ships with guns firing at one another. In the Pacific War, however, the American and Japanese fleets fought one another with aircraft, while the aircraft carriers remained a huge distance apart. At the Battles of the Coral Sea and Midway in 1942, US Navy aircraft inflicted heavy losses, ending the Japanese Navy's control of the Pacific.

Code cracking
US naval intelligence broke the code used for radio messages by the Japanese navy. As a result, they could track the movement of Japanese warships, and in May 1942 were able to intercept ships sent to land Japanese troops at Port Moresby, in New Guinea.

Battle of the Coral Sea
On May 4, 1942, American and Japanese carriers launched aircraft over the Coral Sea to bomb and torpedo each other. The US carrier *Lexington* was sunk, but most of the crew had abandoned ship and were rescued from the sea. Another US carrier, *Yorktown*, was damaged. The Japanese also had one carrier sunk and one badly damaged. The Japanese had to call off their attack on Port Moresby.

***Yorktown* repaired**
Struck by dive-bombers in the Coral Sea, USS *Yorktown* sailed to Pearl Harbor, where it was swiftly repaired. The carrier was sent out again in time to fight at the Battle of Midway in June. The Japanese had not thought the Americans could repair a ship so quickly.

Japanese ships hit at Midway
In June 1942, the Japanese Navy attacked the US base on Midway Island in the Pacific. Forewarned by its code breakers, the US Navy was prepared. The Americans scored a stunning victory, sinking four Japanese carriers and a cruiser. The Japanese lost hundreds of aircraft and their best naval pilots.

Deadly dive-bombers
The devastating damage to the Japanese fleet was inflicted by dive-bombers who dived almost vertically toward the Japanese ships, releasing their bombs, and then pulling steeply upward. The Japanese carriers were packed with fuel and ammunition that exploded when the bombs hit.

Price of success
The Americans also suffered at Midway. *Yorktown* was crippled by Japanese air strikes and was finally sunk by a torpedo from a Japanese submarine. Despite the US losses, Midway was a disaster for the Japanese, and the turning point in the Pacific war.

THE FIGHT BACK BEGINS

In August 1942, the United States and its allies turned from the defensive to the offensive, beginning the long fight to drive the Japanese back across the Pacific. A force of US Marines landed on the island of Guadalcanal in the Solomon Islands. The Marines captured and held an airstrip the Japanese were building, known as Henderson Field. A series of sea, air, and land battles were fought. The campaign ended in an American victory in February 1943, by which time the Japanese had also suffered defeat in New Guinea.

The Marines
Alongside the US Army, the Marines also played a crucial role in the Pacific war. They were experts in amphibious warfare (landings from the sea), which was vital in attacks on islands held by the Japanese. On Guadalcanal they showed what tough fighters they could be, battling at close quarters and surviving with limited supplies.

"Cactus Air Force"
US Marine pilot Joe Foss shot down 26 Japanese aircraft during the Guadalcanal campaign. He was the most successful ace in the "Cactus Air Force"—the nickname given to the airmen based at Henderson Field airstrip. They provided air cover, and this threat of air attack prevented Japanese ships from operating in daylight.

Guadalcanal jungle base
Jungle-fighting presented huge problems. Diseases such as malaria, dengue fever, and dysentery were common. Marines lived in mud-floored huts and fought against Japanese soldiers skilled at concealment.

Captured Japanese soldiers on Guadalcanal

Many soldiers lost their lives in mass *banzai* charges—fight-to-the-death suicide missions—as death was considered preferable to capture. Only 1,000 Japanese were taken prisoner (seen here), but 25,000 were killed.

Desperate contest at sea

The Japanese took to ferrying men and supplies into Guadalcanal by night, on fast warships. The Americans called this the "Tokyo Express." In the five major naval battles fought in the desperate struggle for control of the seas around the island, about 5,000 American sailors and 3,500 Japanese lost their lives.

Australians in New Guinea

While US soldiers battled for Guadalcanal, Australian troops fought the Japanese on the Kokoda Trail in New Guinea. Both sides were decimated by disease and faced nightmarish conditions. Many Japanese troops came near to starvation. With American help, the Australians had turned the tide by January 1943.

Koreans labor for the Japanese
Korea had been a Japanese colony since 1910. During the war millions of Koreans were forced to work for the Japanese as, in effect, slave labor. Hundreds of thousands were brought to mainland Japan to work.

SUFFERING ASIA

THE JAPANESE CLAIMED to be liberating the peoples of Asia from Western imperialists, and called the area they conquered the "Co-Prosperity Sphere." But in practice, they brutally mistreated other Asians, and exploited them as forced laborers. Local people were often left without food and other essentials. Many of the people of British-ruled India also faced hardship.

Chinese suffering
The Chinese people suffered terribly during the war. Millions of civilians died as the Japanese military forces devastated towns and villages. On occasion the Japanese used poison gas in China. They also tried to spread bubonic plague as a form of biological warfare, and carried out cruel medical experiments on Chinese prisoners.

Viet Minh leader
With Paris already occupied, France didn't put up a fight when the Japanese invaded French Indochina. Ho Chi Minh, a Vietnamese communist, formed a resistance movement to oppose them. Called the Viet Minh, it was backed by the US. After World War II, Ho fought the French, and then the US in the Vietnam War.

BENGAL FAMINE

In 1943 a terrible famine struck the Bengal area of British India. Bad weather led to food shortages and, because of the war, the British administration failed to carry out normal famine relief measures. The poorest suffered the most, and several million people are thought to have died from starvation.

About 40,000 Indians served in the Japanese-backed Indian National Army, which fought against the British.

India divided
The British-ruled Indian subcontinent supplied the largest volunteer army in history (2.5 million men, such as these soldiers pictured) to fight for Britain in World War II. However, Indian nationalists still fought for independence, and some, led by Subhas Chandra Bose, even fought against the British.

Indian nationalism suppressed
In 1942 Indian nationalists launched a "Quit India" movement, demanding independence from Britain. The British put down demonstrations and imprisoned thousands of nationalists and nationalist leaders, such as Mohandas Gandhi and Jawaharlal Nehru.

TURNING OF THE TIDE

IN 1942 IT WAS STILL UNCERTAIN which side would win the war. Germany and Japan held vast areas of territory, but the Allies, especially the United States and the Soviet Union, were potentially far more powerful countries. They could produce more tanks, planes, and ships than their enemies. Due to these vast resources, the Allies turned the tide of the war. By summer 1944 it was no longer a question of if the Allies would win, but when.

Invasion of Sicily
British soldiers attack a railroad station on July 25, 1943, during the Allied invasion of Sicily.

May 30
The RAF launches the first thousand bomber raid against Cologne

October 23
British Commonwealth forces take on the Afrika Korps at the Battle of El Alamein, and defeat them by November 2

January 20
At the Wannsee Conference, Nazi officials discuss plans to exterminate the Jews in Europe

August 19
Canadian and British troops suffer heavy losses in an attack on Dieppe

January 14
President Roosevelt and Prime Minister Churchill have a 12-day-long meeting in Casablanca

1942

June 30
In the desert war, Rommel's Afrika Korps drives the British back to El Alamein in Egypt

November 8
American and British troops land in French North Africa

January 31
Encircled German forces surrender to the Soviets at Stalingrad

September 13
Battle begins between German and Soviet forces for control of the Soviet city of Stalingrad

May 13
The war in North Africa ends with the surrender of Axis forces in Tunisia

July 24
British and American bombers destroy much of the German city of Hamburg

May 18
In Italy, Allied troops break through the German defensive line at Monte Cassino

July 10
Allied forces invade Sicily

September 3
Italy surrenders, but German troops resist an Allied invasion of the Italian mainland

February 15
Allied bombers flatten the monastery of Monte Cassino in Italy

June 22
A Japanese invasion of India from Burma is defeated at the Battle of Imphal

1943   1944

May 24
German U-boats are withdrawn from the Atlantic after suffering heavy losses

July 25
Mussolini is dismissed as head of the Italian government

June 6
D-Day: Allied armies land on the coast of Normandy

July 9
US forces complete capture of the Pacific island of Saipan

May 17
RAF Lancaster bombers carry out the "Dambuster" raids on Ruhr dams

July 12
Soviet forces defeat the Germans in a massive tank battle at Kursk

November 28
Roosevelt, Churchill, and Stalin meet for a conference in Tehran

June 19–20
The Japanese navy suffers a crushing defeat in the Battle of the Philippine Sea

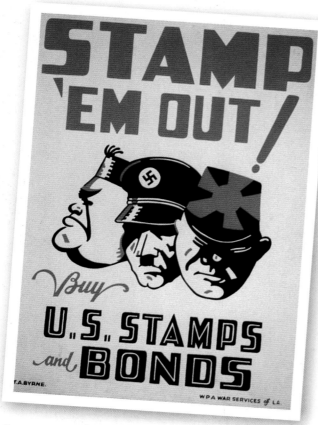

AMERICA GEARED UP FOR WAR

THE KEY TO THE SUCCESS of the United States in the war was its vast industrial capacity and natural resources. American factories turned out huge amounts of every war essential, from warships and aircraft, to trucks, bombs, and shells. Producing these war goods changed American society in significant ways, and made the US, by 1945, by far the richest and most powerful country in the world.

Investing in the war
The American war effort was partly paid for by raising taxes, but the government also borrowed money from American savers, who bought war bonds as a patriotic investment. The bonds raised $18 billion to pay for the war.

Making it last
Many key products were rationed in the United States, including gasoline, meat, tires, and coffee. Production of many consumer goods was banned, so that factories would make arms for the war. Rubber particularly was in very short supply.

Good times
Despite rationing, the war brought good times for many Americans. People who had been unemployed in the Depression years of the 1930s found jobs. Factories competing for workers raised wages. Horse racing was a boom area, as was movie-going—such leisure activities soaked up the spare cash.

Entertaining America at war
The American entertainment industry was eager to show its patriotic support for the war effort. Singers, musicians, comedians, and Hollywood stars entertained the troops. Comedian Bob Hope was a popular performer at shows for the forces.

During the war, US aircraft factories built 18,000 Boeing B-24 bombers and 30,000 Douglas transport planes.

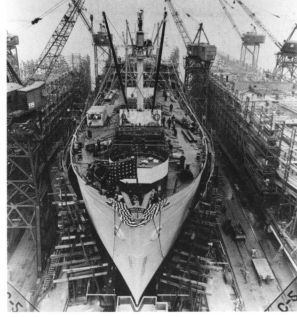

Liberty ships
Mass production of ships and aircraft was the greatest achievement of US wartime industry. More than 2,500 Liberty cargo ships were produced, the largest number of ships of a single design ever made. Whereas a ship normally took a year to build, a Liberty ship took about six weeks. Warships were also made far more quickly than the enemy could sink them. By the end of the war the US Navy had more than 100 aircraft carriers.

Black Americans on the move
The demand for labor brought a major change for African-Americans, most of whom still lived in poverty in the Deep South. Hundreds of thousands moved to the cities of the North and the West Coast, taking jobs that had previously been reserved for whites. They earned more money than ever before, and founded black communities in cities such as Los Angeles.

"American industrial genius has been called upon to bring its resources and its talents into action… We must have more ships, more guns, more planes—more of everything. We must be the great arsenal of democracy."

American President Franklin D. Roosevelt, December 29, 1940

Women contributing to the mass production of bombers in an American aircraft assembly plant during WWII

LIFE IN BRITAIN AT WAR

FACING THE GREATEST CRISIS in their history, the British people responded to the demands of the war with strength and determination. Almost every aspect of their lives became controlled by the government. People were told where they must work, what clothes they could wear, and what they could eat. The British put up with the regulations because the vast majority of them supported the war effort.

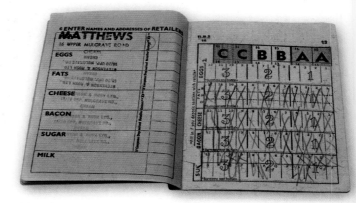

Food rationing

There was strict rationing, setting down how much of different foods a person could have each week. It was the fairest way of sharing goods in short supply. Sugar and tea were early rationed goods, joined later by many others. The ration could be very small—1 ounce (28 grams) of cheese per person per week, for example. The choice was limited, but what food there was proved healthy. Some poor people ate better through rationing than they had before the war.

Dig for Victory

People were encouraged to make up for food shortages by growing their own vegetables. Even Kensington Gardens, next to London's Hyde Park, was turned over to food production.

Utility clothing

Clothing was rationed on a coupon system. Everyone had a ration book with coupons to use in clothing stores. Eight coupons would get a pair of pants, seven coupons a pair of shoes. Clothes were standardized to save on waste. Despite attempts to make utility clothes look glamorous, women found them dull.

Interrupted education

Many children remained in areas bombed by the Germans. Their schools had air raid shelters attached to them. Pupils often had their education disrupted—for example, when their school had been hit by a bomb.

War work

Men and women were conscripted into essential jobs from industry to farming. For example, around 20,000 young men were drafted to work in the coal mines. They were known as "Bevin Boys" after the Minister of Labor Ernest Bevin.

Americans in Britain

Many soldiers from Allied countries were based in Britain. Americans were especially numerous. A lot of British women fell in love with American men and at the end of the war about 80,000 went to live in the US as "GI brides"—wives of American soldiers.

Enjoying life

Although life was hard, people still enjoyed themselves. Most young people went to the movies once or twice a week, enjoying romantic dramas and patriotic war movies. Dance halls were regularly packed, with "Big Band" jazz music providing the favorite rhythm.

Woman power
This famous World War II poster was designed to encourage American women to work in war factories. Millions did just that, doing manufacturing jobs previously thought unsuitable for women. Such factory workers were represented by this image of "Rosie the Riveter."

WOMEN AT WAR

FEW WOMEN FOUGHT IN COMBAT during World War II, but they did "war work" of many kinds. Women did a variety of jobs previously kept for men—from building aircraft to driving trucks. But war also made life hard. Many mothers had to bring up families on their own. For women working outside the home, hours were long and pay was low. In many countries bombing raids, or occupying armies, brought fear and suffering.

When the war in Europe ended, there were nearly seven million women doing civilian war work in Britain.

Nursing the wounded
The most traditional role for women in warfare was nursing. Nurses followed the troops into every theater of war and were often near the front line. Nurses needed the courage to work when under fire.

Working the land
In many countries women did farm work. For example, in Germany, six million women worked the land. In Britain, 80,000 women worked as "land girls"—members of the Women's Land Army.

Controlling the air
About half a million British women joined the armed forces. The roles they fulfilled ranged from cooking and driving, to vital jobs in control and communications. For example, women passed on instructions to pilots engaged in air combat during the Battle of Britain.

Women in uniform
Most women recruited into the armed forces did not take part in combat, but filled vital support roles. In the United States, women could join the WAC (Women's Army Corps) or its naval equivalent, WAVE (Women Accepted for Volunteer Emergency Service).

Japanese workers
World War II brought dramatic change for Japanese women, who had traditionally been treated as totally inferior to men. With Japanese men away serving in the armed forces, women found new jobs in coal mines, arms factories, and steel mills.

Resistance fighters
Women did not usually carry guns in regular armies, but women in resistance movements sometimes did. They fought with men in guerrilla warfare. These Italian women belonged to the group that fought against the Germans and Fascists in northern Italy.

Female pilots
The Soviet Union was the only country to use women pilots in combat. In Britain, women fliers did other jobs, such as taking new aircraft from factories to air bases. Pauline Gower (above) set up the women's section of the ATA (Air Transport Auxiliary).

ALLIED VICTORY IN NORTH AFRICA

IN 1942 THE DESERT WAR in North Africa swung in favor of the Allies. The British Eighth Army stopped Rommel's Afrika Korps in Egypt—first at Alma Halfa and then in the large-scale Battle of El Alamein. As the Afrika Korps retreated, the Allies landed troops in French North Africa (Algeria and Morocco), so the Axis forces found themselves under attack from both sides. The Americans who landed in French North Africa suffered losses, but eventually Rommel was beaten.

Montgomery in charge
In August 1942, the Eighth Army came under the command of General Bernard Montgomery. He raised morale by his lively personality, but was a cautious general who would not attack without careful preparation. He won fame and immense honor for the victory at El Alamein.

Commonwealth effort
The Eighth Army that triumphed at El Alamein was a multinational force. As well as British soldiers, Commonwealth forces played an important part—New Zealanders, Australians, South Africans, and Indian troops. Britain's European allies, including the Free French and the Poles, also contributed.

Battle of El Alamein
The British attack at El Alamein began at night. After heavy gunfire, troops advanced through minefields to take on the Axis powers. The battle lasted days, and for a while it seemed that the British would not break through. But the Eighth Army had twice as many men as its opponents, and the Axis defenses finally cracked.

Desert Air Force

The British RAF made a vital contribution to victory in the desert. Conditions were tough. The pilots lived in tents at desert air strips and the aircraft often got sand in their engines. But enemy forces in the desert had no cover to hide from air attack.

Around 200,000 Allied troops fought at El Alamein, and they had more than 1,000 tanks.

TORCH LANDINGS

US troops waded ashore in French North Africa in three separate landings—in Casablanca in Morocco, and Oran and Algiers in Algeria. The three invasions were nicknamed "Operation Torch" since the landings at Casablanca took place before daybreak.

Axis surrender in Tunisia

Hitler threw more troops into North Africa after El Alamein and the Torch landings. When the British and US forces cornered the Axis troops in Tunisia in spring 1943, more than 200,000 Axis soldiers surrendered.

Hard-fought victory

After the defeat at El Alamein, Rommel succeeded in withdrawing his forces westward. The German and Italian forces fought on for five months after the Allied landings in North Africa, before finally succumbing.

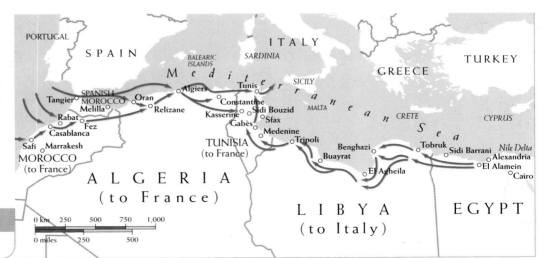

North Africa Campaign

→ Allied advance

FALL OF MUSSOLINI

IN JULY 1943, THE ALLIES INVADED SICILY. For the Italian dictator Mussolini this was a final humiliation and he fell from power. A new Italian government made peace with the Allies and soon changed sides altogether. But German forces took over the defense of Italy and resisted the Allies' invasion of the Italian mainland. Capturing Italy from the Germans proved to be a lot more difficult than any of the Allies predicted.

More than 90,000 *Allied troops were killed in the fighting in Italy from* 1943–1945.

Allied invasion of Italy

→	Allied advance
—	German front line, September 25, 1943
- - -	German front line, March 31, 1944
....	German front line, December 31, 1944

The invasion of Italy

The Allies launched their invasion on Sicily from North Africa. Once they had taken Sicily, British and American forces moved on to make landings in mainland Italy. The Germans blocked their advance northward at a defensive line centered on the monastery of Monte Cassino. Landing troops behind the German lines at Anzio was a failure and Rome did not fall to the Allies until June 1944.

Welcome invasion
The British and Americans invaded Sicily in July 1943, landing the majority of their troops from the sea. They were resisted mostly by German forces, as many war-weary Italians welcomed the invaders rather than fought them.

Fall of Mussolini

Mussolini was dismissed from office by Italy's King Victor Emmanuel III, and was made a prisoner. Eager for peace, most Italians were happy at the news of the dictator's downfall. But people in northern and central Italy immediately fell under German control.

Rescue of Mussolini
German special forces led by Otto Skorzeny rescued Mussolini from captivity in a daring airborne raid. He was taken to lead the Fascists in German-controlled areas of Italy.

Monte Cassino
The bombing of Monte Cassino abbey was one of the most controversial acts of the war. The medieval monastery was at the center of the German defensive position that held up the Allies through the winter of 1943–44. It was flattened by Allied bombers in February 1944. But the bombing did little to help soldiers achieve a breakthrough.

Anzio landings
In January 1944, Allied forces landed at Anzio, between the German lines at Monte Cassino and Rome. But they did not move inland fast enough, and the Germans counterattacked. The Allied landing force proved weak and the battle lasted for several months.

Rome occupied by the Allies
In June 1944, the Germans declared Rome an "open city," letting the Allies occupy it without a fight. Allied troops were greeted as liberators by local people. But the Germans continued the fight in the north of Italy.

STALINGRAD

THROUGHOUT 1942 THE GERMANS ADVANCED deep into the Soviet Union. But in the fall they were involved in a desperate battle for the Soviet city of Stalingrad. With many casualties on both sides, this epic struggle lasted for five months, and ended in a costly defeat for the Germans. After Stalingrad, even most of Hitler's own generals ceased to believe that Germany could win the war.

Street fighting
Soviet troops fought street by street and building by building to stop the Germans from taking control of Stalingrad. Sometimes opposing groups of soldiers held different parts of the same factory or apartment building. The city was reduced to rubble. Most civilians were evacuated; those who remained behind survived as best they could.

Super sniper
The street fighting in Stalingrad was ideal for snipers, who picked off enemy soldiers from hidden positions. One Soviet marksman, Vassili Zaitsev, was credited with 149 kills.

The Stalingrad trap
German troops advanced into Stalingrad, but while they fought inside the city they were surrounded by Soviet forces. Other German troops could not break through to help their colleagues who were caught in a trap. Hitler insisted that they should not retreat, so the Stalingrad army did not try to fight its way out.

SOVIET COMMANDER

The Soviet troops inside Stalingrad were led by General Vasily Chuikov (second from left). He was an energetic and ruthless commander. At the start of the battle he said: "We will defend the city or die in the attempt." No one knows how many Soviet soldiers died in the battle for Stalingrad, but as many as a million may have been killed or wounded.

Flying in supplies

Once the German soldiers in Stalingrad were encircled, they could only be supplied with food and war material by air. *Junkers* transport aircraft flew heroic missions into snow- and ice-covered airstrips, but they could only carry a fraction of what the troops needed.

Paulus surrenders

Field Marshal Friedrich Paulus, the German commander in Stalingrad, surrendered at the end of January 1943. His men were starving and there was no hope they would be relieved. Hitler was angry because he felt Paulus had dishonored the army.

At airstrips outside Stalingrad, some Germans built igloos for shelter in the freezing cold.

Into captivity

About 90,000 soldiers from Germany and its allies were taken prisoner by the Soviets at Stalingrad. They were half-starving and suffering from frostbite. Only about 5,000 survived captivity.

SOVIETS ROLL BACK THE GERMAN TIDE

AFTER THE VICTORY AT STALINGRAD, the Soviet Army drove the Germans back into their own country, clearing the Soviet Union's territory of invading troops within a year and a half. This mighty achievement was bought at an immense cost in human life and war machines. Germany and its allies were also crippled by heavy losses of men and equipment in the massive battles on the eastern front.

Stalin organs
The Soviets used multiple rocket launchers mounted on trucks to bombard enemy troops. They made a terrifying noise and had a devastating effect. The Soviet troops called them *Katyushas* but to the Germans they were "Stalin organs." The *Katyushas* were typical of Soviet equipment—quite simple to operate, easy and cheap to make in large quantities, and impressively effective.

Battle of Kursk
The Battle of Kursk in the summer of 1943 was the world's largest ever tank battle. Altogether, both sides fielded a total of around 6,000 tanks in a battle lasting 10 days. Aircraft attacked from the sky, while tanks fought hard in huge battles that left hundreds of vehicles burned out in the field. The conflict ended in a Soviet victory, even though the Soviets lost more tanks and aircraft than the Germans.

Soviet mastermind

The brain behind the Soviet victories was Marshal Georgi Zhukov. He played a commanding role right through, from the defense of Moscow in December 1941, to the conquest of Berlin in 1945. A tough character, Zhukov stood up to Stalin and stopped the Soviet dictator from interfering too much in war plans.

Tools for the job

The Soviet troops were mostly equipped by their own factories, which achieved astonishing levels of output with often only the most basic machinery, and with workers living in tough conditions. The Soviets were also supplied with equipment by the United States and Britain, especially trucks.

Mixed reception

Soviet forces were welcomed by people who had suffered under the Germans. However, for some the Soviet advance brought grim results. Stalin's secret police took revenge on anyone thought to be a traitor. In the case of the Tatars, an ethnic group living in the Crimea, a whole people was sent to remote parts of the Soviet Union in May 1944, as a collective punishment. Around 100,000 died.

Soviet Advance, 1942–1944

→ Soviet advance
— Soviet front line, December 12, 1942
--- Soviet front line, March 1, 1943
-·- Soviet front line, April 30, 1944
···· Soviet front line, August 19, 1944

Pushing westward

The Soviets advanced in a series of large-scale offensives. Between 1942 and mid-1944 the Soviets pushed the Germans back 930 miles (1,500 km).

FINLAND
Lake Ladoga
Leningrad
Tallinn · Narva
Estonia
Novgorod
Latvia
Riga
Kalinin
Dvinsk
Vyaz'ma
Moscow
Memel
Lithuania
Smolensk
Tula
Kaunas
SOVIET UNION
Minsk
Bryansk
Orel
Bialystok
Nazi-occupied Poland
Brest-Litovsk
Kursk
Belgorod
Khar'Kov
Stalingrad
Kiev
Ukraine
Lwów
Tarnopol
SLOVAKIA
Umam'
Rostov
HUNGARY
Kherson
Sea of Azov
Odessa
Kerch
ROMANIA
Sevastopol
YUGOSLAVIA
Black Sea
BULGARIA

0 km 100 200 300
0 miles 100 200

RAVAGED COUNTRY

As the Soviet forces pressed westward, they found a trail of ruined cities and burned villages. The retreating Germans destroyed all the crops, machinery, and buildings they could. In many places this was a second wave of destruction, since much had been ruined during the German advance in 1941 and 1942.

VICTORY IN THE ATLANTIC

IF GERMANY HAD CUT THE SEA ROUTES linking Britain to North America across the Atlantic, it could have won the war. Between 1941 and 1943, German U-boats sank so many Allied merchant ships that they came close to winning the Battle of the Atlantic. Just in time, the Allied navies sank enough German submarines in the spring of 1943 that they were in effect driven from the ocean.

Vital link
Britain relied on imports by sea for its survival. Without food brought in by merchant ships, the British would have starved. America's ability to intervene in the war depended on being able to ferry men and equipment across the Atlantic. Merchant ships crossing the Atlantic traveled in convoys escorted by warships.

Wolf Packs
German U-boats (submarines) were very effective. They hunted in groups known as "Wolf Packs." A Wolf Pack attacked at night, sinking ships with torpedoes. By diving under water, the U-boats escaped any counterattacks. Conditions for submarine crews in the cramped little boats were very hard, but they had good morale in the "happy times" when they sank lots of ships and mostly escaped unscathed.

Sinking of the *Bismarck*
Britain's Navy prevented German warships from blocking the Atlantic routes. When the German battleship *Bismarck* sailed into the Atlantic in May 1941 it was hunted down. *Bismarck* sank the battle cruiser *Hood*, but was then destroyed by the British fleet.

Cruel sea
Life for merchant seamen was dangerous. A submarine attack always came without warning, making the crew very nervous. If their ship was sunk, many were rescued from the sea by other ships, but thousands of seamen died.

More than 30,000 British seamen lost their lives in the Battle of the Atlantic.

Arctic convoys
In addition to crossing the Atlantic, convoys carried war equipment to the Soviet Union. These "Arctic convoys" were punishing for merchant seamen. Sailors had to cope with freezing weather, as well as German attacks. One convoy, PQ-17, lost 24 of its 36 ships.

ASDIC AND DEPTH CHARGES

British, US, and Canadian escort ships developed techniques for detecting and attacking U-boats under water. Asdic was a device that located U-boats by bouncing sound waves off their hulls. Once the submarine was found, warships dropped depth charges to explode under water and blow them up.

Air patrol
Many things caused a turn around in the Battle of the Atlantic in the spring of 1943. One was better radar, which allowed Allied ships to target U-boats when they were on the surface. Another was the cracking of German naval codes, which alerted the Allies to where U-boats were going to attack. Increased use of aircraft also had a big impact. Many U-boats were sunk by attack from the air.

CODE BREAKERS AND SPIES

ONE OF THE MOST IMPORTANT ASPECTS of any war is intelligence—finding out what your enemy is doing or is going to do. In World War II, information was gathered by having spies in the enemy country, and by intercepting the enemy's radio messages. Radio reports were sent in code, so intercepting them was only useful if you could decode them. The Allies were very good at this, for example, in the famous cracking of the Enigma code at Bletchley Park in England.

Soviet spy
Richard Sorge was one of the most successful spies in World War II. He was a German who posed as a pro-Nazi journalist, while secretly working for the Soviet Union. He was sent to Japan to spy on the Japanese government and the German embassy. Unfortunately, the Soviets ignored him when he told them that Germany was going to invade the Soviet Union in June 1941. He was finally caught and executed by the Germans in 1944.

Enigma machine
The Germans relied on the Enigma machine for encoding radio messages. When information was typed in, rotors and electrical circuits inside the machine scrambled it up and produced a coded message. The Germans thought these codes were unbreakable, but many Allied victories, such as the Normandy Landings, were achieved with the help of Enigma code breakers.

Secret agent
The British and Americans sent secret agents into German-occupied Europe to gather information and help local resistance groups. Violette Szabo was a young agent flown into France in 1944. She led French resistance fighters in sabotage operations. Like many other agents, she was eventually arrested by the Gestapo, tortured, and executed.

The decoding work at Bletchley Park was kept a secret until 30 years after the war ended.

Bletchley Park

Britain centered its Enigma decoding operation at Bletchley Park, in Buckinghamshire, England. Some decoders were chosen to work there simply because they were good at crosswords. These inexperienced individuals supplied a stream of high-quality intelligence known as Ultra. Around 9,000 people worked at Bletchley Park, many of them women.

NEW COLOSSUS

The code breakers had no computers, which had not yet been invented, and had to work through the mass of radio intercepts made every day armed only with a pen and paper. Eventually, scientists built machines to help with decoding. One of these, used in Britain, was called Colossus. Although far less powerful than a laptop, it filled a whole room.

Victim of intelligence

In 1943 American Lightning long-range fighters shot down the aircraft in which Admiral Yamamoto, head of the Japanese Navy, was flying. The admiral died because of the skill of US Navy code breakers, who had cracked Japanese naval codes, which told them exactly where and when Yamamoto was flying.

Tight-knit crews
Bomber aircraft had crews of seven to 10 men
performing different tasks, from the pilot and
navigator, to the men who manned the guns.
They depended on one another for survival and
developed a strong group bond. The crew faced a
serious risk of death each time they flew a mission.

STRATEGIC BOMBING

FROM 1942 THE BRITISH ROYAL AIR FORCE (RAF)
and the United States Army Air Force (USAAF)
bombed Germany in mass air raids. The RAF
attacked by night, while the USAAF made daylight
raids. The Germans defended their country fiercely,
and losses of Allied bombers were heavy. Some of
the air raids had a disastrous effect on German cities.

*More than 35,000 USAAF, and 55,000 RAF, servicemen
lost their lives during three years of air raids on Germany.*

Flying Fortress
The Boeing B-17 Flying Fortress
was the most famous US bomber
aircraft of the war. Their
firepower was supposed to be
enough to shoot down any
German fighters that attacked
them, although in practice there
were too many fast-moving
fighters for the B-17 gunners to
hit them all. The B-17s dropped
large numbers of bombs, trying to
hit precise targets on the ground.

Ball-turret gunner
The most unpleasant position on a B-17 bomber was
that of the ball-turret gunner. He sat hunched up in a
tiny turret underneath the aircraft. Like all the crew he
got very cold flying at high altitude. He had to wear an
oxygen mask to breathe and communicated with the
rest of the crew by an intercom system.

Night attack
The RAF attacked Germany by night, because its bombers suffered heavy losses in daylight. Even at night, many bombers were shot down. Accurate bombing was difficult in the dark, so the RAF often aimed only to hit a general area of a town or city.

"Dambusters"
The most famous operation by RAF bombers was the night attack on the Ruhr dams using "bouncing bombs" that skipped on water. Led by Guy Gibson, the bombers' goal was to destroy the dams and flood Germany's industrial center.

Thousand bomber raids
Some RAF night raids devastated German cities through the sheer mass of bombs dropped. There could be as many as a thousand bombers involved in a single raid. The bombing of the German port of Hamburg, in the summer of 1943, caused a firestorm that destroyed much of the city. Around 50,000 people died, most of them civilians.

"The Nazis entered this war under the rather childish delusion that they were going to bomb everyone else, and nobody was going to bomb them… They sowed the wind, and now they are going to reap the whirlwind."

Sir Arthur Harris, head of RAF Bomber Command

A British Royal Air Force bomber crew stands by its aircraft at a base in Lincolnshire, England, in November 1941

LIFE INSIDE NAZI EUROPE

MOST OF MAINLAND EUROPE was controlled by Nazi Germany for at least part of the war. The Nazis cruely exploited the people under their rule. The Germans took food and suppies from conquered countries, leaving their people hungry, and carried off hundreds of thousands of foreign workers to work in Germany. The SS (Hitler's "protection squad") and the Gestapo (secret police) extended their brutal activities from Germany across the continent.

Keeping normal

At first it seemed to people in Nazi-occupied countries that Germany had won the war. People got on with their lives, which often meant collaborating with the Nazis. French civilians grew used to seeing German officers relaxing in pavement cafes.

Forced labor

Millions of people in conquered countries were forced to work for the Germans. Many were sent to Germany to work in factories and on farms. They worked alongside prisoners of war and inmates of concentration camps. Foreign workers eventually made up around one in five of the German workforce. Many died of mistreatment, or through Allied bombing.

Active collaboration

In most countries there were people who welcomed Nazi victory. Many French Nazi sympathizers volunteered to fight in German uniform (seen here). Some ethnic groups also saw a chance to profit. In Yugoslavia, Croatian nationalists set up their own state, and tortured and massacred their Serb neighbors.

Nazi-occupied Europe, 1942

Germany and German-occupied territory	Allies
Germany's allies or occupied by them	Neutral

ICELAND

FAROE ISLANDS

NORWAY SWEDEN FINLAND

SOVIET UNION

IRELAND GREAT BRITAIN DENMARK

THE NETHERLANDS

BELGIUM GREATER GERMANY

OCCUPIED FRANCE PROTECTORATE OF BOHEMIA AND MORAVIA

SLOVAKIA

SWITZERLAND HUNGARY

VICHY FRANCE

PORTUGAL SPAIN CROATIA ROMANIA

SERBIA

MONTENEGRO BULGARIA

CORSICA ITALY ALBANIA

BALEARIC ISLANDS SARDINIA GREECE TURKEY

SICILY

MALTA CRETE CYPRUS

0 km 500 1,000 1,500
0 miles 500 1,000

Nazi-occupied Europe, 1942

Aside from Britain and part of the Soviet Union, by mid-1942 all of Europe was either controlled by Germany and its allies, or neutral—supporting neither side in the war. Germany's allies—Italy, Romania, and Bulgaria—all changed sides later in the war.

Nazis in the Channel Islands

The Channel Islands were the only part of British territory that came under German occupation. Islanders suffered from lack of food, and many were deported as forced labor. But the local government continued to function.

Nazi brutality

The Nazi SS exercised the same absolute power in the rest of Europe as it did in Germany. People were often arrested in the middle of the night and tortured by the Gestapo, sent to concentration camps, or immediately shot.

Cold and hunger

The Germans took food and fuel from occupied countries to give to their own people. As a result, many places suffered severe shortages. The French had to live on a meat ration that was a third of that in Germany. In eastern Europe thousands of people died from starvation and cold.

Stolen children

The racist Nazis ranked the people they conquered by what they looked like. The blond, blue-eyed Norwegians and Dutch were regarded more positively than Slavs. Under the "Lebensborn program" the SS took some 200,000 blond, blue-eyed Polish children away from their Slav parents to be brought up in Germany as Germans. Most never saw their parents again.

THE HOLOCAUST

ALTHOUGH MANY GROUPS SUFFERED under Nazi rule—including homosexuals and Romany—the Jews suffered the most. Under cover of the war, the Nazis went from the general abuse and casual killing of Jews, to a deliberate attempt at the total extermination of the Jewish population under their control. From all over Europe Jews were transported to death camps in Nazi-occupied Poland simply to be killed. The number of Jews murdered by the Nazis is thought to total around six million. This is known as the Holocaust.

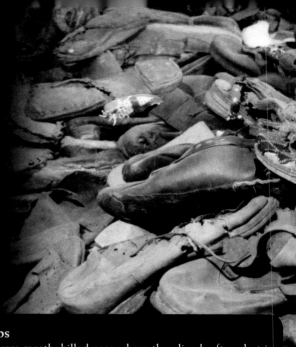

Death camps
At first Jews were mostly killed near where they lived, often shot in front of mass graves. But these killings were unorganized. From 1942 camps were built in Nazi-occupied Poland designed for efficient mass killing. Jews were taken to the camps in overcrowded cattle trucks. There they were herded into gas chambers and killed. Few survived the death camps; for example, of half a million Jews taken to Belzec camp (in present-day Ukraine), only two survived.

Breeding hatred
The Nazis kept up a huge amount of propaganda to convince the German population that Jewish people were responsible for the war. In this poster a caricatured Jew is shown as the evil force behind the Allies, represented by their flags.

Hinter den Feindmächten: der Jude

Slave labor
Germany was short of people to work in its war industries, so thousands of Jews were used as slave labor in factories. Although this was a cruel experience, it often saved them from death, at least for a time. If the Jews became too weak to

Children at Auschwitz
Auschwitz (in Poland) was both a death camp and a work camp. On arrival, Jews considered useful as laborers were taken to work in factories; those not thought useful were sent straight to the gas chambers and killed. Almost all children sent to Auschwitz were killed immediately on arrival. A few survived, mostly because they were used in cruel medical experiments.

ANNE FRANK

Some Jews tried to escape capture by hiding. Anne Frank was one of these. Her family were German Jews living in Amsterdam (in the Netherlands). The Germans occupied the Netherlands in 1940. When they began rounding up Jews, Anne and her family hid in rooms with a secret entrance behind a bookcase. After two years, they were found by the Nazis and sent to Auschwitz. Anne and her sister Margot were later sent to the camp at Belsen, in Germany, where both died. Anne Frank's diary, published after the war, is one of the most moving records of the Holocaust.

Anne Frank (above) wrote her diary while in hiding.

Warsaw ghetto uprising

Most Jews were powerless against their enemies, but they attempted resistance where they could. In 1943 there was an armed uprising by Polish Jews in the Warsaw ghetto. The uprising was crushed by the Nazi SS. About 13,000 Jews died in the fighting. The remaining Jews were rounded up at gunpoint and sent to death camps.

VOICES THE HOLOCAUST

Millions of Jews experienced the horrors of the Holocaust, transported by the Nazis to camps where they were either killed immediately, or ruthlessly exploited as slave labor. Pitifully few survived to tell the story of their sufferings.

"When the transport [train] with people who were destined to be gassed arrived at the railway ramp, the SS officers selected from among the new arrivals persons fit for work, while the rest—old people, all children, women with children in their arms, and other people not deemed fit to work—were loaded on to trucks and driven to the gas chambers. I used to follow behind till we reached the bunker. There people were first driven into the barrack huts where the victims undressed and then went naked to the gas chamber… After driving all of them into the gas chamber, the door was closed and an SS man in a gas mask threw a Zyklon [gas] tin through an opening in the side wall. The shouting and screaming of the victims could be heard through that opening, and it was clear that they were fighting for their lives. These shouts were heard for a very short while…"

Dr. Johann Kremer, German SS doctor at Auschwitz, witnessed these gassings on September 2, 1942. This is his testimony given under interrogation after the war.

"The train traveled slowly with long unnerving halts. Through the slit we saw the tall pale cliffs of the Adige valley and the names of the last Italian cities disappear behind us… Among the 45 people in our wagon only four saw their homes again, and it was by far the most fortunate wagon. We suffered from thirst and cold; at every stop we clamored for water, or even a handful of snow, but we were rarely heard; the soldiers of the escort drove off anybody who tried to approach the convoy. Two young mothers, nursing their children, groaned night and day, begging for water. Our state of nervous tension made the hunger, exhaustion, and lack of sleep seem less of a torment. But the hours of darkness were nightmares without end."

Primo Levi, an Italian Holocaust survivor, describes being transported in a goods wagon from a camp in Italy to Auschwitz in 1944.

"*THE CONDITIONS IN which these people [Jewish victims] live are appalling. One has to take a tour around and see their faces, their slow staggering gait, and feeble movements. The state of their minds is plainly written on their faces, as starvation has reduced their bodies to skeletons. The fact is that all these were once clean-living and sane and certainly not the type to do harm to the Nazis. They are Jews and are dying now at the rate of 300 a day. They must die and nothing can save them—their end is inescapable; they are too far gone now to be brought back to life. I saw their corpses lying near their hovels, for they crawl or totter out into the sunlight to die. I watched them make their last feeble journeys, and even as I watched they died.*"

British soldier Peter Coombs wrote this letter
to his wife on May 4, 1945, after taking part in
the liberation of the camp at Bergen-Belsen.

New arrivals to a concentration camp, still in their own clothes, are forced to parade in front of Nazi guards

"The Jews are the sworn enemies of the German people and must be eradicated. Every Jew that we can lay our hands on is to be destroyed now during the war, without exception."

SS chief Heinrich Himmler gives instructions to Auschwitz camp commandant Rudolf Hess in the summer of 1941

RESISTANCE MOVEMENTS

IN MOST GERMAN-OCCUPIED countries resistance movements were organized to fight Nazi rule. Their activities ranged from gathering intelligence, to sabotage, and full-scale guerrilla fighting. British and American agents were sent in to link up with these movements. If resistance fighters were caught by the Nazis, they faced imprisonment in concentration camps, torture, and death. But they contributed to the Allied victory in Europe and helped restore national pride in countries humiliated by defeat and occupation.

Getting into Occupied Europe
Both Britain and the US sent agents into Occupied Europe, often armed with hidden radios and weapons. They were flown in at night in aircraft such as the Lysander. They ususally landed in countryside fields, where they were met by members of the resistance.

Outstanding agent
Women were often very active in the Resistance, and as Allied agents. Virginia Hall was a one-legged American woman who worked for both the British and the Americans in Occupied France. She was decorated for her work helping organize and supply French resistance fighters.

Norwegian saboteurs
One of the most important resistance operations was the attack by Norwegian fighters on a factory in German-occupied Norway. The factory was producing material that could have been used by Germany in the making of an atom bomb.

COMMUNIST PARTISANS

Communists played a leading role in the Resistance, especially in Italy, France, Greece, and Yugoslavia. However, they also often fought with noncommunist resistance groups. In German-occupied Yugoslavia, for example, a group of communists, led by Josip Broz Tito, mounted a full-scale guerrilla war that tied down large numbers of German troops. But they also fought against the predominantly Serb resistance movement, known as the Chetniks. Tito went on to rule Yugoslavia after the war.

French resistance

By 1944 the French Resistance had grown into a large movement. Many young people joined to escape being sent to work in German factories. In the maquis—the rough, wild country of southern France—they fought a guerrilla war against the Germans, using light weapons such as British-supplied Sten guns.

In 1944, 116,000 armed fighters from the French resistance helped the Allies liberate France.

Resistance hero

Jean Moulin was the most famous French resistance leader. He created a unified movement out of the many anti-Nazi groups that existed in France. Arrested in summer 1943, he was tortured by the Gestapo but died without revealing any secrets.

Nazi reprisals

The Nazis responded to acts of resistance with brutality against local people. In 1942, leading SS officer Reinhardt Heydrich was killed in Prague by Czech resistance fighters. The Nazis responded by massacring all the men living in the Czech village of Lidice. The village was destroyed and the children were carried off by the Gestapo. Out of 105 Lidice children, only 17 survived the war.

POWS IN EUROPE

MILLIONS OF SERVICEMEN of all nationalities were taken prisoner in the course of World War II. Some spent many years in prisoner of war (PoW) camps. The treatment they received varied greatly. For Germans captured by the Soviets, and Soviets captured by the Germans, imprisonment was likely to be a death sentence. On the other hand, most British and Americans kept in German camps, and German and Italian PoWs held in Britain and North America, were handled according to agreed upon rules that made their lives bearable.

Deadly hostility
Nazi Germany and the Soviet Union respected no rules of humanity in their life-or-death struggle. PoWs were kept in awful conditions, poorly fed, cold, and without medical care. Hundreds of thousands died. The Germans worked Soviet PoWs to death as slave labor. They also massacred thousands of them by gassing in camps such as Auschwitz.

Allied PoWs
On the whole, the Germans and Italians dealt with British and American PoWs according to the laws of the Geneva Convention—an international agreement of how PoWs should be treated. Life was certainly very hard for the prisoners, who lived cooped up behind barbed wire. But they were at least allowed to receive food parcels from the Red Cross and letters from home, and were usually under the control of their own officers.

Colditz
The infamous Colditz PoW camp was in a German castle. It was used as a high-security prison to house prisoners who had tried to escape, or were considered dangerous. Despite the increased security, escape from Colditz still proved possible.

Great escapes
Many Allied prisoners tried to escape from their camps. They were usually able to find some way out. But getting to a neutral country without being caught was far more difficult. In March 1944, 76 Allied PoWs escaped from the Stalag Luft III camp in Poland. All but three were recaptured; 50 were murdered by the Gestapo.

More than 2 million Soviet PoWs had died in captivity by early 1942.

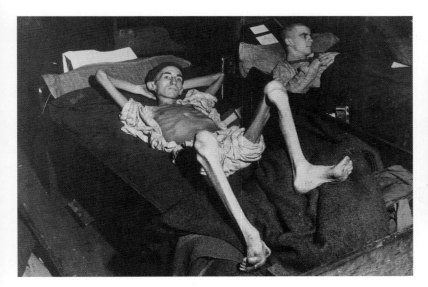

Worsening conditions
The condition of PoWs in Germany got worse in the last year of the war. Food was scarce and prisoners from the Western Allies suffered brutal treatment. Prisoners were also accidental victims of Allied bombing. By the time the war ended, many of those still imprisoned were in poor shape.

Prisoners' chapel
Generally, Axis PoWs held in camps in Britain and the US were reasonably well-treated. There were even complaints in the United States that German PoWs were living in better conditions than many American civilians. One reminder of the large numbers of Italian prisoners in Britain during the war is the Italian Chapel on the remote Scottish island of Orkney, which was built and decorated by PoWs.

117

HOLDING THE ALLIANCE TOGETHER

IT WAS VITAL TO THE ALLIED WAR EFFORT that the major partners—the United States, Britain, and the Soviet Union—should keep on good terms and cooperate with one another fully in defeating the Nazis. These were very different countries, and each was led by a very different kind of powerful individual: Roosevelt, Churchill, and Stalin. Their goals and interests were not the same, but the "Big Three" Allied leaders succeeded in holding the alliance together.

Winston Churchill

British Prime Minister Churchill was the leader of a government that answered to parliament. But in practice he personally ran the war effort from his offices in Whitehall. He worked hard despite his age (he was 70 in 1944), and was popular with the British people even when the war went badly.

Franklin D. Roosevelt

Famous for countering the Depression in the 1930s, US President Roosevelt already had nine years' experience in power by the time the US entered the war. He was the only president ever elected for more than two four-year terms in office—he won his fourth presidential election in 1944.

Joseph Stalin

Soviet leader Stalin was an all-powerful dictator responsible for the deaths of millions of his own people. A suspicious and ruthless man, he did not trust Britain or the US at all. But he saw that the alliance with the West served his interests, and generally kept his part of any deals made with his allies.

Polish problem

A major problem for the Allies was the future of Poland. Britain had entered the war in defense of the Poles, and Polish soldiers and pilots were making a major contribution to the war effort. To maintain good relations with Stalin, Churchill and Roosevelt agreed that the Soviet Union could keep the part of Poland it had seized in 1939. This was seen as a betrayal by Polish troops helping the Allies fight the Germans in Italy.

By the end of the war there were 51 countries in the alliance against Germany and Japan.

Free French leader

Other members of the alliance had little influence over the "Big Three." General Charles de Gaulle, the Free French leader, struggled even to have himself accepted as representing France. But toward the end of the war, de Gaulle had France recognized as one of the major Allied powers.

Meeting in Africa

Despite the danger of moving around the world in wartime, Allied leaders held occasional face-to-face meetings. In 1943 Roosevelt crossed the Atlantic in a flying boat to meet Churchill in Casablanca, in Morocco. There they agreed on the principle of "unconditional surrender"—there would be no peace negotiations with the enemy; they would just have to give in to the Allies.

Teheran summit

The first meeting of all the "Big Three" was held in Teheran, in Iran, in 1943. It was the first time that Stalin had left the Soviet Union since 1917. The Soviet leader was happy because almost all his demands were met.

PREPARING TO INVADE FRANCE

IN 1942 A FORCE made up of mostly Canadian troops crossed the Channel from Britain, to attack the French port of Dieppe, held by the Germans. The attack was a costly failure, and thousands of Canadians were killed or taken prisoner. This taught the Allies just how difficult it would be to land a large invasion force successfully in German-occupied France. It was not until 1944 that Britain and the United States felt strong enough to prepare for an invasion of Normandy.

Eisenhower, supreme commander
American General Dwight D. Eisenhower was put in command of the Normandy invasion. He had American, British, Canadian, and other Allied forces under his control. Eisenhower was a tough but diplomatic man, who kept everyone working together, and he was a strong decision-maker.

Preinvasion buildup
Astonishing numbers of Allied troops, with all their equipment, turned the south of England into an armed camp. They included one and a half million American servicemen. The troops carried out large-scale rehearsals for the invasion, including mass jumps by paratroops, and landings on English beaches from landing craft.

Inflatable tank
The Allies chose Normandy as the place to land their troops, but they wanted the Germans to think that the invasion was intended for Calais, much farther east. Lots of inflatable dummy tanks and fake landing craft made of wood were placed in the area of Britain opposite Calais, where they would be spotted by German aircraft. The Germans were taken in by the deception. Even after the landings in Normandy started, Hitler held troops back expecting the main invasion to come at Calais.

Pluto and Mulberry
Allied scientists and engineers made some amazing equipment for the invasion. One of the most vital was Pluto, an undersea pipeline to carry fuel across the Channel. Another was Mulberry, a floating harbor that was towed across the Channel and anchored off the Normandy coast. Mulberry included floating roadways.

Bombing raids on France

In the first half of 1944 British and American aircraft carried out heavy bombing raids across northern France. They targeted road and rail links so the Germans would not be able to rush in reinforcements. To fit the deception plan, the air forces bombed more fiercely around Calais than around Normandy.

Landing craft

More than four thousand landing craft were assembled in British ports to carry the soldiers and their equipment across the Channel. These craft had flat bottoms so that they could sail close into the sandy beaches.

Strengthening the Atlantic Wall

The Germans knew that an invasion would come one day. From 1942 they built coastal defenses from the French-Spanish border to Norway. This was known as the Atlantic Wall. In 1944, Field Marshal Erwin Rommel toured the defenses. He had them strengthened with obstacles to block tanks on the beaches, and with mines.

Softening up
To prepare the way for the invasion, the Allies bombarded the German defenses from the air and the sea. Six battleships and 19 cruisers pounded the defenders with gunfire. The Germans were shocked and dazed by the attack.

THE D-DAY LANDINGS

ON D-DAY, JUNE 6, 1944, a vast fleet of ships traveled from England to land an invasion force in Normandy, France. Supreme Commander General Eisenhower took a risk in giving the go-ahead to the operation despite the chance of bad weather. The beaches where the men landed were defended by German troops and the Allies had to fight hard to establish themselves on shore.

Airborne troops
The first Allied soldiers to go into Normandy were paratroopers (paras). During the night, while the fleet was crossing the Channel, they dropped by parachute inland from the beaches. The airborne forces suffered losses, but took control of bridges and other key points.

Beach landing
Landing craft carried men as close to the beaches as they could. Then the ramp at the front of the craft was let down and the soldiers waded ashore with their heavy packs and weapons. At Omaha Beach, where the fighting was heaviest, many US soldiers never reached land. They were hit by enemy fire, or drowned in deep water.

D-Day Landings, June 1944

→ British and Canadian landings
→ American landings
— Allied front line, June 6/7

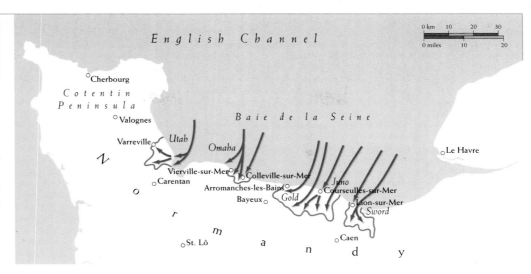

English Channel

Cherbourg
Cotentin Peninsula
Valognes
Varreville   Utah
Vierville-sur-Mer
Carentan
Bayeux
St. Lô

Baie de la Seine

Omaha
Colleville-sur-Mer
Arromanches-les-Bains
Gold
Juno
Courseulles-sur-Mer
Lion-sur-Mer
Sword
Caen

Le Havre

Normandy

0 km 10 20 30
0 miles 10 20

The Normandy beaches

The landings took place on five beaches, codenamed Utah, Omaha, Gold, Juno, and Sword. US airborne troops dropped on Utah Beach, and British paras to the east of Sword. By the end of D-Day, there were almost 150,000 Allied troops in France.

Reinforcing success

Once the Allies had control of the beaches they had to build up their forces in Normandy as fast as possible. They poured troop reinforcements, equipment, and supplies ashore, while the Germans struggled to counterattack. The British and Canadians had lighter casualties than the Americans on D-Day, but suffered in heavy fighting inland over the following weeks.

Allied forces on D-Day included more than 6,000 ships and 13,000 aircraft.

German losses

Allied losses on D-Day have been estimated at around 10,000 men killed or wounded. German losses have never been calculated accurately, but many German soldiers were taken prisoner at the beaches. The Germans had been caught by surprise, partly because the poor weather made them think that an invasion was unlikely. They recovered quickly, however, and fought stubbornly to keep the Allies down near the Normandy coast.

VOICES
D-DAY

On June 6, 1944, around 150,000 Allied soldiers landed on the coast of Normandy, France. For many of these young men, it was their first experience of combat. Wading ashore from landing craft under fire, they had to cope with fear and panic as comrades were killed or wounded around them, and fight their way off the beaches.

"The French coast was in sight and we could see smoke where the big guns on the ships had been firing... The closer we got we could tell that there was trouble. We didn't see any of A Company... the coxswain dropped the ramp and when you open up the ramp on a landing craft, that's when the machine guns open up on you. Captain Zappacosta was first off and he was hit immediately... The next two men off were both hit... and I was the fourth man off. What saved my life was that the boat reared up and I went off the side of the ramp... up to my neck in the water... Zappacosta came up and mumbled something... and he went back down and we never saw him again. I kept looking back at who was following, and they were being cut down just like you wouldn't believe. No one have I ever met until this day who survived that boat."

Bob L. Sales, a Virginian serving with 116th US Infantry, landed on Omaha Beach.

"**S**OLDIERS, SAILORS, AND AIRMEN of the Allied Expeditionary Force! You are about to embark upon the Great Crusade, toward which we have striven these many months. The eyes of the world are upon you. The hopes and prayers of liberty-loving people everywhere march with you. In company with our brave Allies and brothers-in-arms on other fronts, we will bring about the destruction of the German war machine, the elimination of Nazi tyranny over the oppressed peoples of Europe, and security for ourselves in a free world."

General Dwight D. Eisenhower, Supreme Allied
Commander, addresses the troops on D-Day.

"**N**OBODY CAN KNOW what it is like to be on a beach when you can do nothing. When you're under severe fire and you've got to get off and live. People doing it for the first time—no matter how many times you tell them—they don't realize it. And people didn't get off the beach. They were so transfixed with fright, they couldn't get off. I was transfixed with fright, but I had the certain knowledge that you either stopped and died or you got up and got away. So I took the coward's view and got out of the bloody place."

Sergeant William Spearman, an experienced
soldier in the British Army's No 4 Commando,
landed on Sword Beach.

"Two kinds of people are staying on this beach, the dead and those who are going to die. Now let's get the hell out of here!"

US Colonel George Taylor on Omaha Beach

US combat troops wade ashore during the Normandy landings, codenamed "Operation Overlord", on June 6, 1944

THE BURMA CAMPAIGN

BURMA WAS PART OF THE BRITISH EMPIRE. In 1942 Japanese troops invaded Burma and advanced to the border of Assam in British-ruled India. This cut off the "Burma Road," the supply route from India to the Nationalist Chinese army in southwest China. The Allies fought back by sending in special forces by air. From 1944 the Allies drove the Japanese back after hard-fought victories in difficult jungle terrain.

Irregular soldier
Orde Wingate, a major general in the British Army, was a very unusual officer. He was most at home living rough in a jungle or desert. It was his idea to place troops behind enemy lines, a tactic he used in Burma. He was killed in a plane crash in 1944.

Merrill's Marauders
The US equivalent of the Chindits was Merrill's Marauders. Many of the American soldiers recruited for this had fought in other Pacific island battles, which gave them experience of jungle warfare. Led by General Frank Merrill, the Marauders marched 1,000 miles (1,600 km) into the Burmese jungle, where they fought hard against the Japanese.

Wingate's Chindits
Britain created special forces known as the Chindits, led by Orde Wingate. They were a mix of British and Indian soldiers. Several thousand were landed by air in the Burmese jungle to carry out attacks on Japanese forces. Many were killed, either by enemy action or as a result of diseases, but they were effective fighters who successfully harassed the Japanese.

Flying the hump
The Japanese occupation of Burma cut off the Allied supply road to southwest China, so supplies to the Nationalist Chinese had to be flown from Assam, in northern India, across the Himalayas. British and US pilots called this dangerous mission "flying the hump."

Chinese forces
The Chinese Nationalists, led by Chiang Kai-shek, did not want to commit their forces to the risky business of fighting the Japanese. Chinese Nationalist troops were sometimes of poor quality. They often included children as young as 10 years old.

INDIAN NATIONAL ARMY
Indians fought on both sides in the Burma campaign. About 40,000 soldiers of the anti-British Indian National Army (INA) fought on the Japanese side, led by Subhas Chandra Bose. Their goal was to liberate India from British rule. But the INA were outnumbered by Indians who fought for the British.

Fighting at Imphal and Kohima
In 1944 the Japanese attacked northeast India from Burma. At the battles of Imphal and Kohima, British forces drove the Japanese back. Around 50,000 Japanese troops were killed or wounded. It was the turning of the tide in the Burmese war. From then on the Allies took the offensive and Burma was retaken in the course of 1945.

Beach landings
US forces had to land on Pacific island beaches under heavy fire from the Japanese. Although they were well trained in making landings from ship to shore, many men died. At Tarawa, a coral island, the US landing ships got stuck on the reef and men had to wade ashore from far out. Many were killed or injured before they reached the beach.

ISLAND-HOPPING ACROSS THE PACIFIC

THROUGH 1943 AND 1944 the US Marines led an advance across the Pacific, hopping from island to island to get closer to Japan. The Japanese Navy could not stop the American troops from reaching the islands, but soldiers defended each island with heroism. The result was a series of fierce battles, notably at Eniwetok, Tarawa, and Saipan. Eventually, the Japanese were beaten, but casualties on both sides were heavy.

Amphibious vehicles
The Americans had a range of clever vehicles that could "swim" ashore and then work on land. LVTs (Landing Vehicles Tracked) were lightly armored and landed on shore from the sea, then drove up the beach. They could fire on the enemy while sheltering the soldiers inside. They were also known as "alligators."

NAVAJO "CODE-TALKERS"

The US Marines used Native American Navajos to radio messages during the island battles. The Navajo language, known to only a few people, was used as a military code. When the Japanese heard messages by the Navajo "code-talkers," they found them impossible to work out.

Ferocious battle at Saipan

The fighting for Saipan, an island in the Marianas, in the summer of 1944, was very fierce and ruthless. The Japanese retreated into caves in the island's volcanic mountains, where they held out for three weeks. The Americans used heavy artillery and flame-throwers in their attempts to clear the caves.

Rare surrender

The Japanese soldiers on Saipan showed great bravery when faced with almost certain death. They had been taught that it was wrong to surrender, and were ordered to fight to the death. Of 30,000 Japanese soldiers on Saipan, only 900 were taken prisoner. The rest died.

Mass suicide

The last surviving Japanese troops on Saipan mounted a suicidal final charge in which almost all were killed. Around 22,000 Japanese civilians also died, many preferring to commit suicide rather than become prisoners. Japanese women even jumped off cliffs holding their children in their arms. They were told by Japanese officers it was their patriotic duty to die.

Taking prisoners

Guy Gabaldon was a Mexican-American who had been brought up by a Japanese-American family. As a Marine on Saipan, Gabaldon used his knowledge of the Japanese language to talk to the Americans' enemy. He is credited with saving the lives of at least 800 Japanese soldiers and civilians by persuading them to surrender.

US NAVAL TRIUMPH IN THE PACIFIC

THE KEY TO AMERICA'S SUCCESS in the Pacific was the power of its navy. In two major battles in 1944—the Philippine Sea and Leyte Gulf—the once proud Japanese Navy was crushed and humiliated. The Japanese were at times able to inflict damage on their enemy, but their own losses were always much heavier. Unlike the Americans, they could not replace the ships and men that they lost. Japanese airmen were forced to use suicide bombing to have any impact on the US fleet.

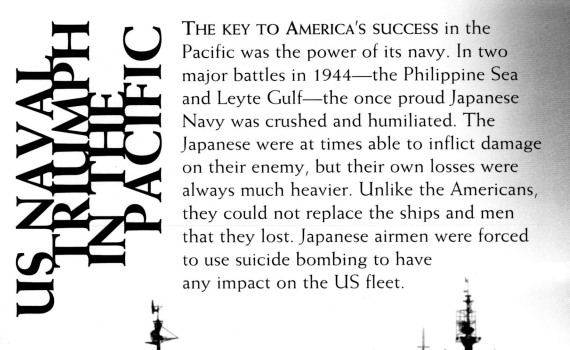

Carrier power
By 1944, the US had built many new aircraft carriers that were grouped into Carrier Task Forces. These were very powerful, capable of putting hundreds of aircraft into the air at one time. The carriers were defended from air attack by anti-aircraft guns on other warships.

The Marianas Turkey Shoot
Japanese and US aircraft carriers were used against each other in the Battle of the Philippine Sea in June 1944. Japanese aircraft attacked the American fleet, but hundreds were shot down. The battle was so one-sided that the Americans called it the "Marianas Turkey Shoot"— shooting turkeys being a very simple activity.

Hellcat fighters

American success was partly down to having more skillful pilots than the Japanese, who had lost many of their best pilots in earlier battles. It was also a result of the Americans' new aircraft. From 1943, US carriers had Grumman Hellcat fighters, which did battle with Japanese Zeros. Hellcats shot down more than 5,000 Japanese aircraft.

The Japanese Navy had 90 percent of its ships sunk or damaged in the Pacific war.

Battle of Leyte Gulf

The Japanese made a last attempt to destroy the American fleet during US landings on the Philippines in October 1944. The result was probably the largest naval battle in history. More than 200 US warships and around 70 Japanese ships took part. The battle was a catastrophe for the Japanese, who lost 27 ships and 10,000 men. American losses were lighter but still severe—six warships sunk and 3,500 men killed.

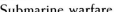

Submarine warfare

American submarines were used to deadly effect in naval battles with Japan. The submarines also sank many Japanese cargo ships. After Leyte Gulf, Japan could no longer import materials such as oil and food by sea. The country faced starvation and its war effort was crippled by lack of fuel for its surviving ships and aircraft.

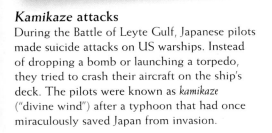

Kamikaze attacks

During the Battle of Leyte Gulf, Japanese pilots made suicide attacks on US warships. Instead of dropping a bomb or launching a torpedo, they tried to crash their aircraft on the ship's deck. The pilots were known as *kamikaze* ("divine wind") after a typhoon that had once miraculously saved Japan from invasion.

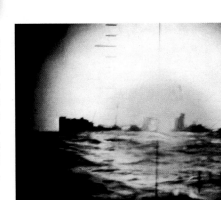

ENDGAME

THE LAST YEAR OF THE WAR was immensely destructive as Germany and Japan fought to the death against overwhelming odds. Many who had suffered under Nazi or Japanese occupation experienced the joy of liberation. But hundreds of thousands died as cities were bombarded by aerial attacks, culminating in the dropping of atom bombs on Japanese cities. After fierce battles, the Allies achieved total victory, both in the European and Pacific theaters of war.

Dresden devastated
The German city of Dresden lies in ruin after the Allied bombing raids of February 13–15, 1945. The city was destroyed and tens of thousands of people lost their lives.

August 1
Resistance fighters in Warsaw launch an uprising against the Germans, which is crushed after two months of fighting

September 17
Allied paratroopers are dropped in the Netherlands at the start of Operation Market Garden

January 13
Soviet forces begin advancing into Germany from the east

July 20
An attempt to assassinate Hitler fails

September 3
The Belgian capital Brussels is liberated

November 7
Roosevelt is reelected US President for a record fourth term of office

February 13–14
Allied bombers destroy the German city of Dresden

1944

August 24
Paris is liberated by Allied forces

October 26
The US Navy inflicts a crushing defeat on the Japanese at the Battle of Leyte Gulf after three days of fighting

January 27
Auschwitz is liberated

February 19
US Marines land on the island of Iwo Jima

September 8
German V-2 missiles are fired at Britain for the first time

December 16
The Battle of the Bulge begins; the battle ends in German defeat the following month

February 4
The Allied leaders Stalin, Churchill, and Roosevelt meet at Yalta

April 28
Former Italian dictator
Benito Mussolini is
captured and killed by
Italian resistance fighters

August 6
The United States
drops an atom bomb on the
Japanese city of Hiroshima

April 1
American forces land on
Okinawa; the battle for the
island continues into June

May 7
German commanders
sign a general surrender

July 17
Allied leaders attend a
meeting at Potsdam that
lasts until August 2

August 9
Soviet forces invade Japanese-
occupied Manchuria; the Americans
drop a second atom bomb on the
city of Nagasaki

1945

April 12
Roosevelt dies; he
is succeeded as
US president by
Harry S. Truman

May 2
Soviet forces complete
the conquest of Berlin

July 26
British Prime Minister Churchill is
defeated in a general election and
replaced by Clement Attlee

August 14
Japan agrees to
surrender

March 9–10
US B-29 bombers raid Tokyo,
starting a firestorm that destroys
a large part of the city

April 30
Hitler commits suicide
in his bunker in Berlin

May 8
VE Day
(Victory in Europe)

September 2
Japan signs a formal
surrender on board the
US battleship *Missouri*

135

→	Allied advance
—	German front line, July 25
- - -	German front line, August 13
–·–·–	German front line, August 26
·····	German front line, September 14
········	German front line, December 15

Western front, June–Sept 1944
Allied forces broke out from Normandy in early August, and advanced with great speed across France and Belgium. Their main problem was that supplies of fuel could not keep up with their advancing tanks. There was a separate landing of Allied forces on the southern coast of France, in mid-August.

THE LIBERATION OF FRANCE AND BELGIUM

THE ALLIED TROOPS HAD A TOUGH FIGHT after D-Day. They were stuck in the zone around the landing beaches in Normandy. It took two months for them to break out. When they did, though, their tanks raced across France, liberating Paris, and driving on into Belgium. It looked like Germany might be defeated by Christmas.

Tank commander
American General George Patton led the rapid Allied tank charge across France. He was famous for his aggressive spirit and was nicknamed "Old Blood and Guts."

Destruction of Caen
The city of Caen was only 6 miles (10 km) inland from the Normandy coast, but the Germans held it against the British and Canadians for a month after D-Day. Allied bomber aircraft pounded the city, which was eventually captured on July 9.

Parisian resistance
As the Allies got close to Paris, French resistance fighters emerged and fought the Germans in the streets. About 1,500 resisters died, but they managed to gain control of most of the city.

There was a darker side to liberation. After the Germans left, French resistance fighters took revenge on those alleged to have sided with the Nazis. Thousands were shot and many more imprisoned or publicly humiliated. French women who had associated with German soldiers had their heads shaved.

Free French triumph
General de Gaulle's Free French army were the first Allied troops to enter Paris. De Gaulle led a victory parade through the city after the liberation, and became head of the French government.

Joyous liberation
Wherever Allied forces advanced, they were met by cheering crowds. In the Belgian capital Brussels, liberated on September 3, civilians climbed on to British tanks, waving their national flag, celebrating the end of Nazi occupation.

GERMANY PREPARES TO FIGHT TO THE DEATH

BY THE SUMMER OF 1944, Germany was facing certain defeat. Yet the Nazi leadership had no intention of surrendering. Once an attempt to assassinate Hitler had failed, it was clear that the war would be fought to the bitter end. Although there was some opposition to the Nazis in Germany, they succeeded in rousing German soldiers and civilians to fight on in defense of the homeland, despite a steeply rising death toll.

Assassination attempt

In July 1944, a group of German army officers and diplomats plotted to kill Hitler. A bomb, placed by Colonel von Stauffenberg, exploded in a room where Hitler was holding a meeting, but he survived without serious injury. The plotters committed suicide or were rounded up, tortured, and executed. Hitler later showed Mussolini the bombed-out room.

Life in devastated cities

Allied bombing, devastatingly effective after mid-1944, destroyed German cities. Raids came by day and night, and many died. Those who were not killed or wounded suffered from fear and loss of essential services. Food was scarce, and survival a daily struggle.

Speer revives war effort

Albert Speer was in charge of German war production. He increased output of weapons by exploiting foreign workers, prisoners, and Jews as slave labor. German workers also had to work longer hours. Factories were moved underground or into caves to avoid the bombs.

German Home Guard

As Germany ran short of soldiers, all men between the ages of 16 and 60, who were not already in uniform, were called up for service in the *Volkssturm*, a sort of Home Guard. They were quickly thrown into frontline service during the final defense of Germany.

Hitler Youth

Membership of the Hitler Youth had been compulsory for 14- to 18-year-olds since before the war. During the war, the movement was active in the defense of German cities against air attack. They manned anti-aircraft guns and worked in fire and rescue services. Some Hitler Youth boys went on to fight in frontline army units.

Women conscripted

Hitler held out against forcing women into factories or the armed forces, believing their place to be in the home. But, in late 1944, he accepted that their labor was needed. Women mostly helped with civil defense; for example, some worked as Air Raid Precaution Wardens.

THE WHITE ROSE

Some young Germans rejected the Nazi system by "dropping out" into gang cultures and listening to banned American popular music. A few tried to organize political resistance. This photograph shows members of the White Rose group, students at the University of Munich, who published anti-Nazi leaflets. Most of the group were arrested in 1943, and six were executed.

SEARCH FOR THE MIRACLE WEAPON

FACING DEFEAT, HITLER PUT HIS FAITH in the idea that a "miracle weapon" would turn the war in his favor. In fact, by 1944–45 new inventions, such as ballistic missiles and jet aircraft, were beginning to transform the nature of warfare. But it was the United States, not Germany, that developed the true "miracle weapon," with the atom bomb project [see pages 158–159].

Scientific exiles
Germany was a country with a great scientific tradition, but by the time the war started, many top scientists, including Albert Einstein, had fled to Britain or the United States to escape the Nazis. Losing scientists was one of the main reasons Germany never came close to making an atom bomb.

V-1 flying bombs
The "Doodlebug" was a simple but effective weapon that Germany used from the summer of 1944. It was a pilotless aircraft with explosives packed in its nose. It flew until its engine cut out and then dropped to the ground, exploding on impact. Thousands of V-1s were targeted to hit London.

Flying bomb damage
The V-1s were more frightening for Londoners than The Blitz. Arriving at any time of the day or night, they caused large-scale damage and thousands of deaths, mostly between June and September 1944. After a while, British air defenses got better at shooting the V-1s down, away from populated areas.

Rocket scientist
Wernher von Braun was the head of the German rocket program that developed the V-1 and V-2 bombs. At the end of the war, von Braun and his team were taken to the US to work, developing missiles. They made a major contribution to the US space program—all of today's space rockets are descended from the V-2.

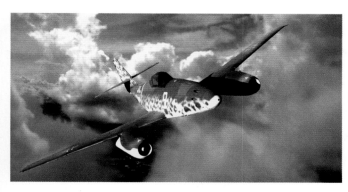

Jet fighter aircraft
When World War II started, all aircraft were driven by propellers, but jet engines were being developed in Britain and Germany. In 1944 the Germans used the first jet aircraft in combat. These *Messerschmitt Me-262s* were faster than any propeller-driven aircraft and shot down quite a few Allied planes. But they were basic and had lots of fatal crashes.

During a two-week period in June 1944, V-1 flying bombs killed or injured 6,000 people in the London area.

GAS WARFARE
During the war, Germany developed deadly nerve gases such as Sarin, a drop of which could kill. However, it was not used because Germany feared retaliation from the Allies—who in fact did not have nerve gas. Neither side in the European war used poison gas, meaning the gas masks given out at the start of the war were never needed. But Japan did use poison gas against the Chinese.

V-2 rockets
The V-1 was followed by the V-2, a ballistic missile—rockets that are initially powered, but then use gravity to reach their target. V-2s were supersonic (faster than the speed of sound), which meant they struck without warning. Fortunately for Londoners, Hitler had only a limited number of V-2s, and many of them fell in the countryside because of faulty guidance and targeting.

PROPAGANDA AND MORALE

As the conflict dragged on, governments presented information about the war to the public in a way that would encourage support for the home nation, and increase hatred of the enemy. Using a mixture of truth and distortion to provide information is known as propaganda. Entertainment was also used to try and raise morale in these difficult times.

During the war, some 90 million Americans went to the movies every week.

Master of propaganda
The most skillful propagandist of all was probably Hitler's right-hand man, Joseph Goebbels. A fanatical Nazi, Goebbels was a master of radio broadcasting, the most effective medium in pre-television times.

Blaming the Jews
This pro-Nazi French poster promotes Hitler's absurd belief that the Jews were to blame for the war. It shows a Jewish man behind Roosevelt, and claims that the Jews were "stealing" North Africa from France.

The Japanese snake
In the US the posters reflected the intense hatred felt toward the Japanese enemy. This poster, encouraging Americans to donate scrap metal to the war effort, shows Japan as a snake.

WAR PHOTOGRAPHERS

War photographers accompanied the armed forces to supply images of the fighting to newspapers and magazines. Among the most famous were the American woman photographer Lee Miller and Hungarian-born Robert Capa. War photographers often took immense risks—Capa landed with troops on Omaha Beach during the fiercest of the fighting on D-Day.

Real-life heroes

Some army men, such as Wing Commander Guy Gibson (far left) who carried out the Dambuster raids, were used for propaganda. They were forced to make public appearances, but were often unhappy at being singled out as heroes. Gibson requested a return to combat and was killed in action in 1944.

At the movies

During the war, movies were vital for keeping people informed. Millions went to movie theaters to watch newsreels as well as feature films. Many wartime movies had a patriotic theme. The famous playwright Noël Coward wrote and starred in the naval drama *In Which We Serve*, a hit movie of 1942.

Soviet strength

The Soviet Union emphasized the wise leadership of Stalin and the unity of the Soviet people. Posters often celebrated the great strength of the country's army. Here the spider of fascism is ruthlessly crushed.

Keeping them happy

Entertainers were used to boost morale. Band leader Glenn Miller and comedian Bob Hope helped to keep Allied troops and civilians smiling. British singer Vera Lynn (shown here) was known as "The Forces' Sweetheart."

THE SOVIETS ADVANCE ON GERMANY

ALTHOUGH SOVIET FORCES had driven the Germans out of most of the Soviet Union by the summer of 1944, they still faced German resistance. The German army never cracked, despite great pressure. Soviet troops suffered heavy casualties as they pushed westward. In former German-occupied Poland, they uncovered evidence of the horrors of the Nazi Holocaust, but the Soviets also carried out their own atrocities against civilians. Many German refugees fled to escape the Soviets' progress.

Warsaw uprising
In the summer of 1944, the Polish resistance (Home Army) began an uprising against the Nazi occupiers. The Home Army was loyal to the Polish government-in-exile in London, which was hostile to the Soviet Union. Soviet forces did not support the uprising, and even prevented the Western Allies from aiding the resistance fighters.

The Eastern Front, 1944

- ➔ Soviet advance
- —— German front line, June 22
- - - - German front line, July 25
- –·–·– German front line, September 25
- ········ German front line, December 15

Soviet advance
From the summer of 1944 through the winter of 1944–45, the Soviet Army recaptured Lithuania, Latvia, and Estonia, and invaded eastern Poland, Romania, Hungary, Bulgaria, and Yugoslavia. The communist partisan leader Tito was allowed to take the Yugoslav capital Belgrade and establish control of the country.

Defeat of the uprising
The Nazi SS ruthlessly put down the Warsaw uprising, killing around three-quarters of the Home Army fighters. The total Polish death toll was over 200,000. The Germans emptied the city of its entire population, sending around 150,000 Polish survivors to labor or concentration camps.

Fleeing from the Soviets
Millions of German civilians fled westward as the Red Army advanced, rightly fearing that the Soviets would take revenge for the terrible suffering inflicted by the Germans on their own people. In one incident, the liner *Wilhelm Gustloff* was sunk by a Soviet submarine, killing around 9,000 refugees, making it the worst sea disaster in history.

Soviet troops found 7,500 prisoners alive in Auschwitz camp in January 1945—at its peak the camp had held 150,000 prisoners.

Liberation of Auschwitz
The Nazis tried to destroy evidence of their crimes, but at Majdanek in July 1944 the Soviets found gas chambers. When Soviet troops liberated Auschwitz in January 1945, only a small number of inmates were still there. Most had been killed or forced to leave with their German guards.

Death marches westward
As they retreated, the Germans made prisoners from their camps leave with them. The forced marches in midwinter caused the deaths of many thousands of already weakened Jews.

GERMANY HOLDS ON IN THE WEST

IN SEPTEMBER 1944, there were hopes that Allied forces advancing across France and Belgium would be able to invade Germany by the end of the year. But the failure of Operation Market Garden, a bold attempt to attack Germany by going through the Netherlands, meant Europe had to endure another winter of war. The Germans even managed a last counterattack, which was defeated during the Battle of the Bulge.

Operation Market Garden
Planned by British Field Marshal Montgomery, Operation Market Garden, launched in September 1944, involved dropping troops by parachute to seize a series of key bridges in the German-occupied Netherlands. Allied tanks would advance overland to join them and the way would be open for an invasion of Germany. But the last bridge at Arnhem was not taken and the operation failed.

Aerial assault
Thousands of British paratroopers (paras) and US airborne forces took part in Operation Market Garden, with troops landing by glider as well as parachute. The sight of massed parachutists descending from the air on the Netherlands was impressive. But airborne troops were at a disadvantage once on the ground, lacking heavy guns or vehicles to help them fight.

Paras at Arnhem
British paras were expected to take the last bridge over the Rhine River at Arnhem. Faced by strong German forces, they suffered heavy casualties in desperate fighting inside the town. Eventually, the survivors either escaped or surrendered.

Battle of the Bulge

In December 1944, Hitler sent his tanks through the Ardennes, intending to break through the Allied lines and sweep up to the coast at Antwerp, Belgium. Taking the Allies by surprise, the attack seemed to be succeeding, but vigorous fighting by the Allies drove the Germans back.

The Battle of the Bulge was the costliest battle of the war for the Americans—around 19,000 US soldiers died.

Defense of Bastogne

During the Battle of the Bulge, the Germans failed to capture the key American-held fortress at Bastogne. When they called on General McAuliffe, the US commander, to surrender, he replied "Nuts!" American troops fought with great bravery in terrible winter weather conditions, against a better-equipped enemy.

Allied air superiority

The German offensive began in midwinter when heavy cloud kept Allied aircraft on the ground. But once the skies cleared, Allied rockets targeted German tanks and trucks.

German tanks crippled

The German panzers (tanks) showed skill and strength, advancing quickly. But they needed to seize Allied fuel dumps because, by this stage of the war, Germany was short of oil supplies. However, the panzers failed to capture Allied fuel and their offensive literally ran out of gas. Hundreds of German tanks were destroyed.

INVADING GERMANY

By FEBRUARY 1945, Germany lay at the mercy of its enemies, yet Hitler still refused to surrender. With almost total command of the air, Allied bombers reduced German cities to rubble. But any sympathy that might have been felt for the Germans was lost with the increasing evidence of Nazi mass murder uncovered by Allied troops.

Summit at Yalta

In February 1945, Stalin, Churchill, and Roosevelt met at Yalta in Ukraine and agreed on the future occupation of Germany and the founding of a United Nations organization to maintain world peace after victory.

Invading Germany, 1945

→ Western Allied advance	— Western Allied front, May 7
→ Soviet advance	— Soviet front line, May 7
— German front line, Apr 1	
--- German front line, Apr 20	

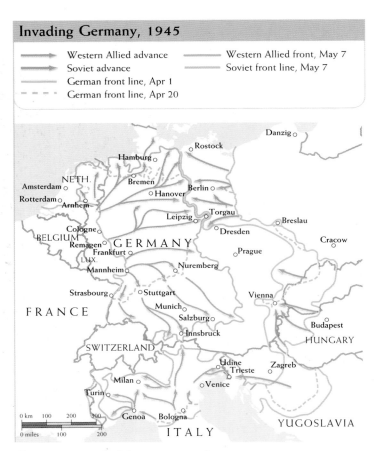

Germany invaded from east and west

The last great obstacle to Allied armies in the West was the Rhine River. After this was crossed in a series of operations in March 1945, Allied troops poured across Germany. They also advanced north through Italy. The Soviets fought their way westward, meeting up with the Western Allies and encircling Berlin.

Bombing of Dresden

The destruction of the historic city of Dresden by Allied bombers in February 1945 was one of the most controversial actions of the war. The city was packed with German refugees fleeing from the east. A firestorm killed at least 25,000 people and possibly many more.

African-Americans

Black Americans played a large part in the fighting in Germany. To be taken prisoner by a black soldier was a special humiliation for Germans taught by the Nazis to believe blacks were racially inferior.

DEATH OF ROOSEVELT

US President Roosevelt did not live to see the victory over Germany for which he had worked so hard. His death on April 12, 1945, was a huge shock and his funeral was an occasion of great public mourning. Roosevelt was succeeded by Harry S. Truman.

Shocking images from Belsen

Allied troops were shocked by what they discovered in Nazi camps as they advanced. The liberation of the camp at Belsen, packed with dead and dying prisoners, mostly Jews, had a profound impact on world opinion. Graphic images brought home the sheer awfulness of Nazi rule.

Russian and US troops meet

Soviet troops advancing from the east, and American troops from the west, met on friendly terms in the center of Germany, at Torgau on the Elbe River, on April 25, 1945. By agreement between the Allies, the task of capturing Berlin was left to the Soviets.

FALL OF THE DICTATORS

Grim birthday

Hitler celebrated his 56th birthday in his Berlin bunker on April 20, 1945. He emerged briefly to meet some of the defenders of Berlin, including boys of Hitler Youth. Hitler wrote a last testament in which he blamed the German people for letting him down, and described the massacre of the Jews as a great achievement. This photo was taken a month before his last birthday.

THE WAR IN EUROPE ENDED with the battle for Berlin, one of the fiercest combats of the entire conflict. Soviet troops encircled the city and fought their way in street by street. Trapped in a bunker in the center of the city, Hitler chose death rather than capture. Germany's military leaders then surrendered.

Death of Hitler

When Soviet soldiers entered Hitler's bunker (pictured here) on May 2, 1945, no trace of the Nazi leader remained. Hitler had married his mistress Eva Braun on April 29 and the couple had committed suicide the following day.

Soviet victory

The Soviet flag was raised on the *Reichstag* building (German parliament) on the same day that Hitler committed suicide, while fighting was still going on. The capture of the city cost the Soviets around 300,000 men. Around 100,000 German soldiers and civilians were also killed. Berlin lay in ruins.

By the time he died, Hitler had wiped out around two-thirds of Europe's Jews.

Death of Mussolini

Two days before Hitler's death, Italian dictator Mussolini was killed. His body, along with those of other Fascists, were hung upside down in a gas station in Milan.

German surrender

Once Hitler was dead, German forces began to give in. This photograph shows Admiral Friedeburg surrendering to Field Marshal Montgomery on May 4, 1945. The final unconditional surrender was signed on May 7, 1945.

Victory celebrations

VE (Victory in Europe) Day was celebrated in London, New York, and other Allied cities on May 8. Street parties were held in many places, but the war with Japan continued.

"The Nazi ringleaders who imagined
themselves the rulers of the world have
found themselves ruined. The mortally
wounded Fascist beast is breathing his last…
The last storming of the Nazi den is on."

Soviet leader Joseph Stalin, May 1, 1945

THE WAR DRAWS NEAR TO JAPAN

Landing on Iwo Jima
The battle for the small volcanic island of Iwo Jima showed how costly the final defeat of Japan might prove. US Marines landed on the island on February 19, 1945. Over the next five weeks the Americans suffered 26,000 casualties as they fought the Japanese.

As AMERICAN FORCES DREW CLOSER, Japanese resistance became more desperate, and American losses mounted. The rise in the numbers of troops, aircraft, and ships sent by the United States and its Allies made Japan's position hopeless. Yet, although they knew they were facing defeat, many in the Japanese government continued to favor fighting on to the death. The Americans planned to invade the Japanese mainland in November 1945 to bring the war to an end.

BALLOON ATTACK

From the fall of 1944, the Japanese launched 9,000 balloon bombs across the Pacific toward the United States. They were paper balloons filled with hydrogen, with explosive devices hung underneath. About 1,000 reached the US, but only one caused casualties, killing a woman and five children. They were the only people killed on mainland America by enemy action in the war.

Battle for Okinawa
From April to June 1945, the Americans fought a ferocious battle for possession of the island of Okinawa, which they intended to use as a base for an invasion of the Japanese mainland. There was intense fighting on land, in the air, and at sea. The use of flame-throwers to clear Japanese out of holes in the rocky terrain was one of the most horrifying aspects of the fighting.

Kamikaze attacks

The Allies assembled a vast fleet to support the Okinawa landings. These warships suffered mass suicide attacks by *kamikaze* pilots. More than 30 ships were sunk by Japanese *kamikaze* aircraft crashing onto their decks.

Piloted bomb

The Japanese even developed a piloted bomb, the *Ohka* ("Cherry Blossom"). The bomb was dropped from an aircraft and steered by the pilot onto its target.

Suffering cilvilians

In the battle for Okinawa, around 150,000 of the island's civilian population died, along with almost 70,000 Japanese soldiers. The Americans suffered more than 50,000 casualties. The suffering on Okinawa seemed to show what would happen if the US Army invaded the Japanese mainland.

Incendiary raid on Tokyo

By the spring of 1945, US B-29 bombers were carrying out mass air raids on Japanese cities. They dropped incendiary bombs (designed to start fires). Most Japanese houses were made of wood, so fires spread easily. In March 1945, a firestorm destroyed a large part of Tokyo. As many as 100,000 people died.

"Among the Americans who served on Iwo Jima, uncommon valor was a common virtue."

Fleet Admiral Chester W. Nimitz

Six American soldiers are photographed raising the US flag atop Mount Suribachi on Iwo Jima, on February 23, 1945

IN SEARCH OF FINAL VICTORY

BY SUMMER 1945, it was clear that Japan had lost the war. Its cities were being destroyed by air attacks, its population was facing starvation because of a naval blockade, and its armed forces were powerless against the great strength of their enemy. But still the Japanese were defending their homeland against an Allied invasion. Desperate to bring Japan to surrender, the Americans prepared to use a terrible new weapon: the atom bomb.

By the war's end, some Japanese children as young as 14 were drafted into the army.

THE MANHATTAN PROJECT

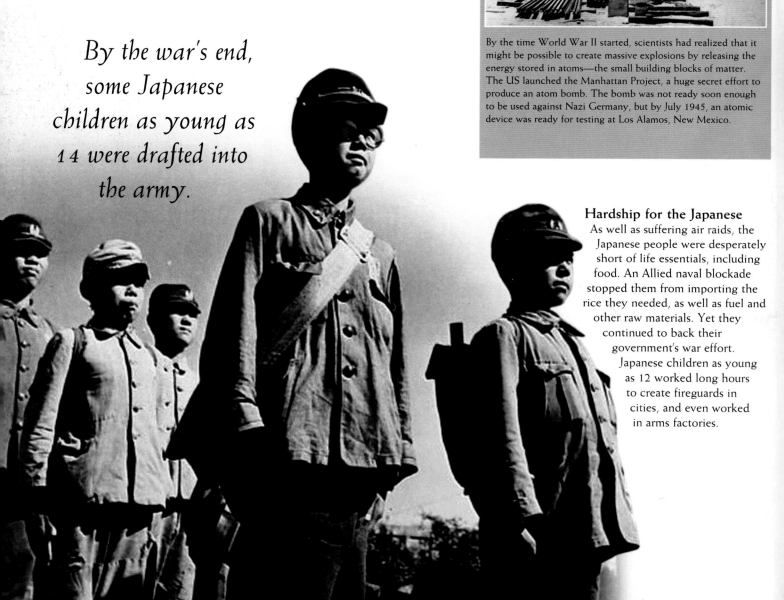

By the time World War II started, scientists had realized that it might be possible to create massive explosions by releasing the energy stored in atoms—the small building blocks of matter. The US launched the Manhattan Project, a huge secret effort to produce an atom bomb. The bomb was not ready soon enough to be used against Nazi Germany, but by July 1945, an atomic device was ready for testing at Los Alamos, New Mexico.

Hardship for the Japanese
As well as suffering air raids, the Japanese people were desperately short of life essentials, including food. An Allied naval blockade stopped them from importing the rice they needed, as well as fuel and other raw materials. Yet they continued to back their government's war effort. Japanese children as young as 12 worked long hours to create fireguards in cities, and even worked in arms factories.

First atomic explosion

In July 1945, scientists carried out a test explosion of the first atomic device. Its power was even greater than they had expected. This photo was taken 16 milliseconds after the explosion was triggered. US President Truman told Stalin that he had a new superpowerful bomb, but Stalin already knew about it from his spies at Los Alamos.

Meeting at Potsdam

By July 1945, when the Allied leaders met at Potsdam in Germany, Truman had replaced Roosevelt as US President. During the meeting, British Prime Minister Churchill was replaced by Clement Attlee. Relations between the Western Allies and the Soviet Union were poor, but Stalin pledged to join in the war against Japan.

Emperor Hirohito

By summer 1945, Japanese Emperor Hirohito wanted to negotiate a peace deal with the Americans. But the US had no intention of negotiating with the Japanese—they wanted a full surrender. Some diplomats thought the United States should at least offer to allow the emperor to stay on his throne if the Japanese surrendered, but the Americans did not want to make any concessions.

Potsdam Declaration

At the end of the Potsdam meeting, Truman and his Allies issued a warning to Japan, threatening them with "prompt and utter destruction" if they did not accept unconditional surrender. The Japanese rejected the demand and so the dropping of the atom bomb was cleared to go ahead.

JAPAN SURRENDERS

BY AUGUST 1945, the Japanese government had still not decided to surrender. But then the US dropped atom bombs on the cities of Hiroshima and Nagasaki, and Soviet troops invaded Japanese-held Manchuria. On August 10, the Japanese told the Americans they would surrender if the emperor could stay on the throne. Some Japanese wanted to fight on, but Emperor Hirohito told them to "bear the unbearable." On August 14, Japan accepted defeat.

Enola Gay
The first atom bomb was carried by a B-29 bomber, called Enola Gay, that took off from a base on the Pacific island of Tinian. The crew flew 1,500 miles (2,400 kilometers) to Hiroshima in clear weather and dropped the bomb at 8:15 on the morning of August 6.

Hiroshima destroyed
The devastation at Hiroshima was unlike anything seen before. The heat and light of the explosion killed thousands of people in under a second. The firestorm killed many more. Thousands later became ill through exposure to nuclear radiation and died more slowly. The total death toll was between 80,000 and 140,000.

The second bomb

On August 9, a second atom bomb was dropped on Japan. The Americans intended to destroy the city of Kokura but the B-29 could not find the target in bad weather and so dropped the bomb on Nagasaki instead. Nagasaki was hilly, so some areas were sheltered from radiation and blast. The death toll was lower than in Hiroshima at between 35,000 and 70,000.

Shock of surrender

Emperor Hirohito announced the surrender on the radio. Army officers who wanted Japan to fight on tried to stop the broadcast, but they failed. The emperor told his people that "the war situation has developed not necessarily to Japan's advantage." Japanese wept in the streets in shock at the surrender.

The Hiroshima atom bomb was nicknamed "Little Boy," and the Nagasaki bomb was referred to as "Fat Man."

Celebrating victory

VJ (Victory over Japan) Day was celebrated with even greater joy than the victory over Hitler three months before. This time the war was really over. Especially relieved were soldiers who had been preparing for the invasion of Japan. But despite the celebrations, the revelation of the awesome power of the atom bomb was a shock to people in Allied countries. They realized they might one day suffer the same fate as Hiroshima and Nagasaki.

Formal surrender

Japan's formal surrender took place on the US battleship *Missouri* on September 2, 1945. Some isolated individuals took much longer to hear the news, and were still fighting for the Japanese emperor in the jungles of Pacific islands and southeast Asia many years later.

VOICES
HIROSHIMA

The people of Hiroshima and Nagasaki are so far the only humans to experience attack with nuclear weapons. When the first atom bomb was dropped on Hiroshima on August 6, 1945, the victims had no idea what had happened to them.

"*An airplane as pretty as a silver treasure was flying… in the sky. I watched it for a while with my hand shading my eyes. Somewhere a voice said: 'Hey, look, it's a parachute!' I looked where the person pointed. That's when it happened. Just where I was looking the sky exploded with an indescribable light. I was instantly thrown hard to the ground and things were raining down on my head and shoulders. Everything was pitch black… I threw off pieces of wood and roof tile, but they kept falling and piling up on me. When I finally struggled free there was a terrible smell and I rubbed my face and nose with a towel I carried around my waist. All the skin peeled off my face, and all the skin on my hands was peeling off and hanging strangely… Such a bright morning until a moment ago. What could have happened? Now we were under a thin cover of darkness, just like dusk.*"

Futaba Kitayama was a 33-year-old woman living in Hiroshima. She was working in a street one mile from where the bomb exploded.

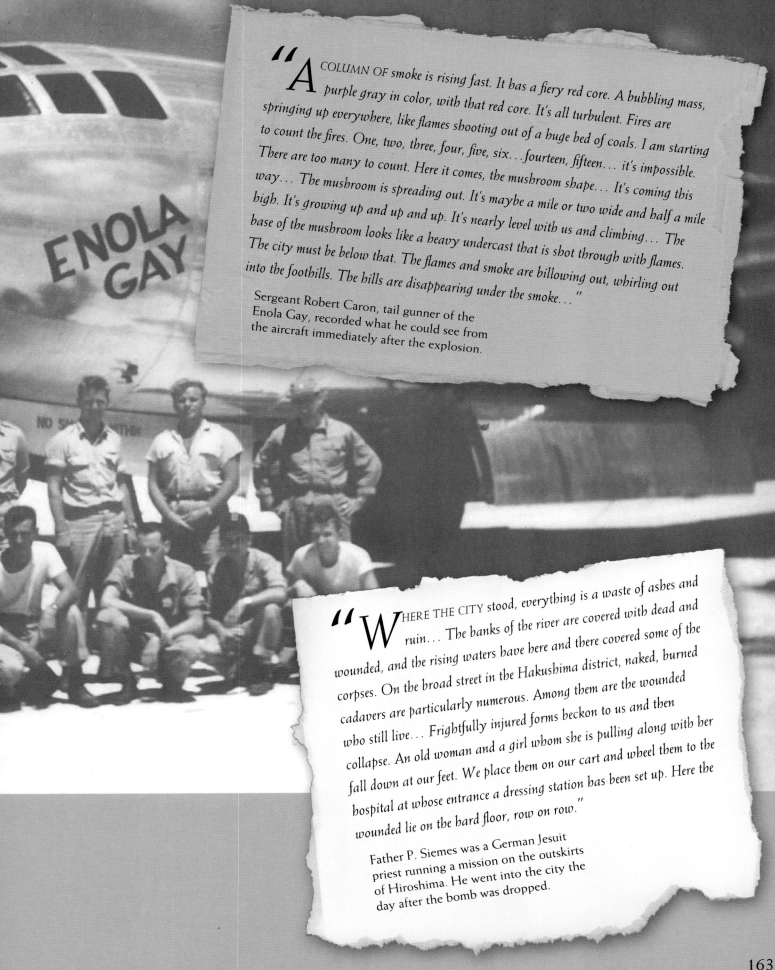

"A COLUMN OF smoke is rising fast. It has a fiery red core. A bubbling mass, purple gray in color, with that red core. It's all turbulent. Fires are springing up everywhere, like flames shooting out of a huge bed of coals. I am starting to count the fires. One, two, three, four, five, six...fourteen, fifteen... it's impossible. There are too many to count. Here it comes, the mushroom shape... It's coming this way... The mushroom is spreading out. It's maybe a mile or two wide and half a mile high. It's growing up and up and up. It's nearly level with us and climbing... The base of the mushroom looks like a heavy undercast that is shot through with flames. The city must be below that. The flames and smoke are billowing out, whirling out into the foothills. The hills are disappearing under the smoke..."

Sergeant Robert Caron, tail gunner of the Enola Gay, recorded what he could see from the aircraft immediately after the explosion.

"WHERE THE CITY stood, everything is a waste of ashes and ruin... The banks of the river are covered with dead and wounded, and the rising waters have here and there covered some of the corpses. On the broad street in the Hakushima district, naked, burned cadavers are particularly numerous. Among them are the wounded who still live... Frightfully injured forms beckon to us and then collapse. An old woman and a girl whom she is pulling along with her fall down at our feet. We place them on our cart and wheel them to the hospital at whose entrance a dressing station has been set up. Here the wounded lie on the hard floor, row on row."

Father P. Siemes was a German Jesuit priest running a mission on the outskirts of Hiroshima. He went into the city the day after the bomb was dropped.

The Japanese city of Hiroshima was reduced to ruins and rubble by the mighty force of the atomic bomb

"Sixteen hours ago an American airplane dropped one bomb on Hiroshima... It is an atomic bomb... The basic power of the universe has been loosed against those who brought war to the Far East... If they do not now accept our terms they may expect a rain of ruin from the air."

US President Truman, August 5, 1945

THE AFTERMATH

AT THE END OF WORLD WAR II, Germany and Japan were utterly defeated and occupied by Allied troops. But true peace proved hard to achieve. The wartime Allies soon fell out, and the United States and the Soviet Union engaged in a "Cold War," building up large stocks of nuclear weapons. The desire of people in Asia and Africa for independence from imperial rule led to further conflicts. Yet, by the end of the millennium, at least some of the wartime hopes for freedom, democracy, and prosperity had been achieved.

Counting the cost
A family places flowers on the grave of an unknown British soldier who was killed at Monte Cassino. After World War II, graves like this existed all over Europe.

March
Civil war breaks out in Greece between communist guerrillas and the British-backed Greek government

February 25
The communist party takes control of Czechoslovakia ending democratic government

April 4
NATO (the North Atlantic Treaty Organization) is founded

June 25
Communist North Korea invades South Korea

March 5
Soviet dictator Joseph Stalin dies

August 30
An Allied Control Council is set up to govern Germany

August 15
India and Pakistan become independent of British rule

October 7
The Soviet zone of Germany becomes the German Democratic Republic (East Germany)

April 28
The US ends its military occupation of Japan

| 1945 | 1946 | 1947 | 1948 | 1949 | 1950 | 1952 | 1953 |

November 20
Nuremberg war crimes trial begins

March 12
The Truman Doctrine commits the US to resisting the spread of communism worldwide

May 23
In Germany, the American, British, and French occupation zones become the Federal Republic of Germany (West Germany)

October 25
Chinese troops enter the Korean War, clashing with UN forces

July 27
A ceasefire ends the war in Korea

March 5
Winston Churchill warns of an "iron curtain" dividing Europe in a speech in Fulton, Missouri

June 24
The Soviet Union imposes a blockade on Berlin

November 1
The United States tests the first hydrogen bomb

March 8
The first US combat troops
are sent to fight in Vietnam;
American troops remain until 1973

May 9
West Germany
joins NATO

March 25
Six European countries form
the Common Market, forerunner
of the European Union

August 20
The Soviet Union and its
allies invade Czechoslovakia
to stop democratic reforms

October 3
Germany is
reunified

| 1955 | 1956 | 1957 | 1961 | 1965 | 1968 | 1989 | 1990 |

November 4
An anticommunist uprising
in Hungary is suppressed
by the Soviet army

August 17
The Berlin Wall is built,
dividing communist-ruled
East Berlin from West Berlin

November 9
The opening of the Berlin
Wall signals the fall of communism
in Eastern Europe

May 14
Responding to NATO, the
communist countries of
Central and Eastern Europe
sign the Warsaw Pact

May 10
Paris peace talks begin between US chief
negotiator Averell Harriman, and North
Vietnamese Foreign Minister Xuan Thuy

167

THE COST OF WAR

THE COST OF WORLD WAR II in human terms was staggering. Between 50 and 70 million people lost their lives in the conflict worldwide. Even in the countries on the winning side, once the victory parades ended, governments faced a desperate struggle to rebuild and recover. Millions of individuals, whose lives had been brutally disrupted by the war, sought a new beginning.

Shortages of everything
Food shortages were serious in many parts of the world, including most of Europe. In Britain, rationing and shortages of fuel were more severe after the war than they had been during it. At the same time, Britain had to provide food and fuel to keep the German population alive in the British-occupied zone of Germany.

Destruction of buildings
There was a severe shortage of housing wherever bombing or shelling had battered cities. Rebuilding would take many years. In the meantime, people often lived in the basements of ruined buildings or in temporary shelters among the ruins.

Refugee camps
Tens of millions of people were homeless refugees at the end of the war. In Europe, these included Jews who had survived the Holocaust and Germans who had left Eastern Europe. Displaced Persons (DPs) were often forced to live in camps, like the one shown here in Berlin, for many years.

Jewish exodus

Many refugees found new homes outside Europe. A flood of Jewish Holocaust survivors headed for British-ruled Palestine. Britain, trying to keep the peace between Jews and Palestinian Arabs, resisted Jewish immigration. The ship *Exodus*, with 4,500 Jewish refugees on board, was turned back from Palestine in 1947.

Return of soldiers

Men who had fought in the war were obviously delighted to return to their families, but coming home was difficult. Families had to learn to get used to each other again. Some men arrived home traumatized by their war experiences.

Around 13 million Germans became refugees in the war and the postwar years.

Prosperous America

The situation in the United States was very different from Europe and much of Asia. The US had not suffered damage on its home territory and its economy had grown spectacularly during the war. In addition to a hero's welcome, returning GIs were given money by the government so they could go to college or buy houses.

DEATH TOLL

No one will ever know exactly how many people died in the war. The Soviet Union had the highest losses, with possibly 25 million soldiers and civilians killed. Around 20 million Chinese may have died in the war. Some 400,000 US servicemen were killed. Germany lost 7 million, of which 2 million were civilians. Around 2.7 million Japanese died. Italy and France each had around half a million war deaths. About 450,000 British died, around 61,000 of them civilians.

DEALING WITH THE DEFEATED

THE MOST URGENT POSTWAR problem for the wartime Allies was how to handle the occupation of Germany and Japan. There was no armed resistance to Allied occupation forces in either country, as people focused on the daily struggle for survival. The Allies prosecuted German and Japanese "war criminals" and, to varying degrees, evicted Nazis from positions of authority. Getting new governments working in the defeated countries took several years.

Military occupation
Germany was divided into American, British, French, and Soviet occupation zones. The former German capital Berlin, which was in the Soviet zone, was also divided into four. The Soviets and the Western Allies could never agree on how best to run Germany.

Germany's "Year Zero"
The Germans called 1945 "Year Zero" because life had been reduced to bare survival. German people lived in ruined houses, with little food or heating. Millions searched for contact with loved ones, who might be in prisoner of war (PoW) camps or hospitals, or could be dead. In bombed cities, women were employed clearing rubble by hand.

German prisoners of war
Millions of German soldiers were held in PoW camps, like this one in Norway. Death rates for PoWs in Soviet hands were very high. Those in camps run by the Western Allies had a better chance of survival. Prisoners in Western-run camps were sent home fairly quickly, but many German PoWs in the Soviet Union were not released until the 1950s.

Nuremberg Trials
Leading Nazis were tried by the International Military Tribunal at Nuremberg, in Germany. Eleven were found guilty, as this poster, produced during the trials, shows (*schuldig* means "guilty" in German). All eleven were sentenced to death, but one of them, Hermann Goering, killed himself before he could be hanged.

Vichy leaders prosecuted
France carried out its own prosecutions of those who had collaborated with the Nazis. The head of the wartime Vichy government, Marshal Philippe Pétain, and his prime minister Pierre Laval, were both put on trial. In this courtroom scene, Pétain is seated and Laval standing. Both were condemned to death, but Pétain's sentence was reduced to life imprisonment.

A large number of Nazis escaped to South America after the German defeat, and were never prosecuted for their crimes.

Japan under MacArthur
General Douglas MacArthur led the American occupation forces in Japan, and he set about trying to create a democratic government in the country. As in Germany, prominent war criminals were prosecuted. General Hideki Tojo was among those executed for war crimes, but there was little assistance for Japanese struggling to rebuild their lives.

"We must make clear to the Germans that the wrong for which their fallen leaders are on trial is not that they lost the war, but that they started it."

Robert H. Jackson, US chief counsel for the prosecution at the Nuremberg Trials

WARTIME ALLIES FALL OUT

WHEN THE WAR ENDED, there were hopes that the wartime Allies would continue to work together to build a peaceful future, but these hopes were soon dashed. There were basic differences between the Soviet Union and the Western Allies that led to distrust and hostility. Europe was soon divided between countries to the east, dominated by the Soviet Union, and countries to the west, mostly allied to the United States. With large armed forces they faced one another across an "iron curtain."

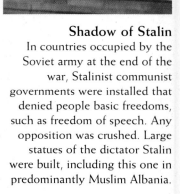

Shadow of Stalin
In countries occupied by the Soviet army at the end of the war, Stalinist communist governments were installed that denied people basic freedoms, such as freedom of speech. Any opposition was crushed. Large statues of the dictator Stalin were built, including this one in predominantly Muslim Albania.

United Nations founded
The United Nations (UN), founded in 1945, was intended as a bigger, better version of the prewar League of Nations. The major wartime allies, as permanent members of the UN Security Council, were supposed to run the postwar world in peaceful cooperation. However, maintaining world peace proved impossible.

Iron curtain
Winston Churchill was the first major statesman to talk publicly of the breakdown in relations with the Soviet Union after the war. In a speech at Fulton, Missouri, in March 1946, he said Europe was divided by an "iron curtain" between east and west.

Greek civil war

In several countries outside the Soviet-controlled areas, including France, Italy, and Greece, communist parties had a lot of popular support. Greek communists fought a guerrilla war against a government backed by Britain and the US. The Greek communists were defeated in 1949. By that time, the Italian and French communist parties had also lost out in democratic elections.

NATO FOUNDED

The North Atlantic Treaty Organization (NATO) was founded in 1949, tying the United States to the defense of Western Europe. As a result of this alliance, American troops and aircraft were permanently stationed in Europe, and American nuclear weapons, targeted at the Soviet Union, were set to be used if the Soviets attacked a Western European country. The US also provided massive economic aid to Western Europe.

Postwar Europe

European borders mostly returned to where they had been in the mid-1930s. Poland shifted westward at the expense of Germany, losing territory in the east to the Soviet Union, which also absorbed Estonia, Lithuania, and Latvia. Britain, the US, and France created West Germany out of their occupation zones, while the Soviet zone became communist-ruled East Germany. The "iron curtain" ran through the center of Germany.

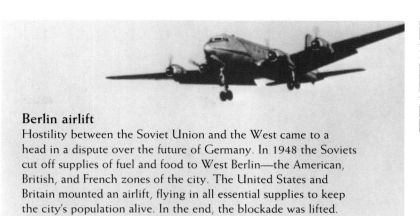

Berlin airlift

Hostility between the Soviet Union and the West came to a head in a dispute over the future of Germany. In 1948 the Soviets cut off supplies of fuel and food to West Berlin—the American, British, and French zones of the city. The United States and Britain mounted an airlift, flying in all essential supplies to keep the city's population alive. In the end, the blockade was lifted.

European Allegiances

— Iron curtain
◼ Original NATO countries (in 1949)
◼ Warsaw Pact countries
◻ Neutral or nonaligned countries

WORLD IN TURMOIL

OUTSIDE EUROPE, MUCH OF THE WORLD was plagued by warfare in the postwar period. The weakness of the European imperialist countries—especially Britain and France—encouraged nationalists in their empires to seek independence, sometimes by force. The United States committed itself to a global role of resistance to the spread of communism, but communists nonetheless took power in China. By 1950 a major war was being fought in Korea.

Truman Doctrine

In 1947, President Truman committed the United States to stopping the spread of communism worldwide. He announced that the US would resist armed aggression by the Soviet Union or its allies, and try to stop communists from coming to power in any country. This was known as the Truman Doctrine.

Indian independence

Many people in the empires still ruled by European powers wanted independence after the war. India, Pakistan, and Ceylon (Sri Lanka) became independent from Britain in 1947. Although marred by violence between Muslim and Hindu communities, this new freedom was enthusiatically celebrated.

Mao's civil war victory

In 1949 Chinese communist forces, led by Mao Ze Dong, won a civil war against Chiang Kai-shek's Nationalists. Mao created a strong government in mainland China, but the Nationalists remained in control of the island of Formosa (Taiwan).

Independence wars

In many places the European powers fought to resist giving their colonies independence. Britain fought wars in Kenya, Malaya (Malaysia), and Cyprus. The French were driven out of Indochina in 1954 after a war with the communist-led Viet Minh. This poster celebrates the Viet Minh victory.

Fighting for the UN in Korea

Korea was divided after World War II, with a pro-Soviet government in the North and a pro-American government in the South. In 1950 communist North Korea invaded the South. The United Nations—without the Soviet Union—backed sending in US-led forces to defend South Korea.

At the time of Stalin's death in 1953, about one-third of the world's population was in communist countries.

Chinese head for Korea

Communist China sent a large army into Korea to fight the American-led UN forces. The war cost more than 3 million lives. By 1953 the fighting ended with Korea still divided between North and South along almost exactly the same border as at the start of the war. It remains divided to this day.

FOUNDATION OF ISRAEL

In the postwar years, Jews in Palestine fought a war both against the British army and against Palestinian Arabs. In 1948 the British withdrew from Palestine and, in May, the UN recognized Israel as a country in its own right. Following this declaration, Israel was immediately attacked by neighboring Arab states, which strongly opposed Israeli independence.

POSTWAR PROSPERITY

BY THE 1950S, countries such as Britain, France, West Germany, Italy, Japan, and the United States were entering an economic boom that would bring prosperity for the majority of their people. There was no return to the mass unemployment and poverty that had been common before the war. At the same time, many social groups faced a long, hard struggle to achieve equal rights in the postwar world.

Back to home and babies
After the war, women in North America and Europe mostly returned to the home. Security was highly prized and a postwar "baby boom" occurred as people sought satisfaction in family life. The fight for equal rights for women only began in earnest in the 1960s.

Army service
In the US and Britain, the unsettled world situation meant that many young men were conscripted into the armed forces long after the war had ended. Even singer Elvis Presley had to do his military service.

Black civil rights
The contribution of African-Americans to the US war effort received little reward. Many blacks were thrown out of their well-paid jobs when white workers returned from war. The democratic rights for which the war had been fought were still denied to most African-Americans. Black people campaigned with growing energy for full civil rights.

Benefits of growth

In Western Europe, governments pledged to provide social security and full employment for their people. These policies largely succeeded and workers were better off than ever before. Money was spent on washing machines, cars, and televisions.

COMMON MARKET

The experience of two world wars made French and German leaders determined to end the hostility between their countries. From 1958, meetings between French President Charles de Gaulle and West German Chancellor Konrad Adenauer formed a new relationship based on cooperation. France and West Germany were key founders of the Common Market, the forerunner of today's European Union.

Booming Japan and Germany

Through the 1950s, Japan and West Germany made a spectacular recovery from wartime destruction. By mass-producing goods, such as these Volkswagen cars, using the most up-to-date methods, they dominated the world's export markets. The living standards of the Germans and Japanese rose dramatically as a result.

THE COLD WAR

FOR 40 YEARS AFTER WORLD WAR II, people feared there would be another world war, fought between the US and the Soviet Union. This threatened global destruction, because of the existence of nuclear weapons. Fortunately, the conflict between the Americans and the Soviets remained a "Cold War" (without military action). The Cold War ended in the late 1980s.

Nuclear arms race
After the Soviet Union exploded its own atom bomb in 1949, the Soviets and the Americans began a race to develop bigger and more effective nuclear weapons. The hydrogen bomb, first tested in 1952, was far more powerful than the bomb that had destroyed Hiroshima.

Mutually assured destruction
By the 1960s, the Americans and the Soviets had enough nuclear weapons to destroy one another's cities. Missiles with nuclear warheads were ready and waiting to fire, and there was no defense against them. If war broke out, both sides faced massive damage. The certainty of mutual destruction stopped them from fighting a world war.

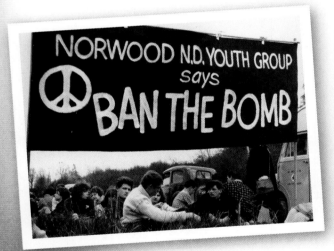

Peace movements
There was widespread support for world peace, especially with the possibility of nuclear war. Movements such as the Campaign for Nuclear Disarmament (CND), founded in Britain in the 1950s, protested against the nuclear arms race.

War in Vietnam

The United States did resort to war to resist the spread of communism. Between 1965 and 1973, American forces fought a large-scale war to stop South Vietnam from coming under communist control. The war cost 50,000 US lives and was a failure—communist North Vietnam eventually took over the South.

Soviet tanks sent in

Communist governments in Soviet-occupied parts of Europe relied on Soviet military force to keep them in power. Revolts demanding freedom and democracy, as in Hungary in 1956 and Czechoslovakia in 1968, were put down by Soviet tanks.

ENEMIES BECOME FRIENDS

Germany and Japan, America's enemies in World War II, turned into valuable allies of the US in the Cold War. Japan stayed mostly disarmed, but it provided support for American policy in Asia from the Korean War onward. West Germany became a member of the NATO military alliance in 1955. East Germany was an ally of the Soviet Union.

Fall of the Berlin wall

The wall built by the communists in 1961 to seal off East from West Berlin became the symbol of the Cold War division of Europe. In 1989 the fall of the Berlin wall marked the overthrow of the communist regimes in Eastern Europe. The two halves of Germany were reunited in 1990.

REMEMBERING WORLD WAR II

WORLD WAR II IS REMEMBERED in the victor countries as a story of triumph over evil. The British, for example, celebrate their resistance to Hitler in 1940 as their "finest hour." As the world entered a new millennium, and those who personally remembered the war grew old, young people continued to be reminded of the war by public ceremonies, and by movies and TV programs.

Holocaust memorials
The victims of the Holocaust are commemorated by many museums and monuments. The exhibit above is part of the Holocaust memorial that was opened in Berlin in May 2005. The concentration camp at Auschwitz, Poland, which has been the scene of many acts of remembrance, was declared a World Heritage Site in 2006.

Hiroshima remembered
The city of Hiroshima is in one way an example of how the war is forgotten. Once a completely ruined place of death, within 10 years of the war's end it was a bustling city again, with few visible signs of what had happened there. But the city's "Peace Park" has become the site of annual peace ceremonies.

Katyn Memorial

Facing up to the past could be a reluctant acceptance of guilt. It was only in 1990 that the Russians accepted responsibility for massacring Poles at Katyn. Memorials, like this one in Warsaw, record the crime, but no Russians were ever prosecuted as war criminals as a result.

JAPANESE DENIAL

Japan has been reluctant to admit responsibility for aggression and atrocities in World War II. In 1995, on the 50th anniversary of the war's ending, Prime Minister Murayama did accept that Japan had committed faults, but his statement was very controversial. In particular, Japan still denies carrying out the massacre at Nanking, a stance that outrages China.

America's national World War II memorial in Washington, D.C., opened in 2004, 59 years after the end of the war.

The war on screen

Steven Spielberg's movie *Saving Private Ryan*, which started with the D-Day landings, was made in 1998. Its success showed the continuing fascination with the war in popular culture. Even comedy programs, such as *The Simpsons* and *Family Guy*, often make references to World War II. Germany's ability to confront its past was shown by the success of the 2004 movie *Downfall*, about Hitler's last days in his Berlin bunker.

D-Day remembered

More than half a century after the war's end, veterans still met to remember major events, sharing pride in what they had done. The veterans here are commemorating the 60th anniversary of D-Day in 2004.

The American cemetery in Luxembourg houses the remains of around 5,000 American soldiers, most of whom died in the Battle of the Bulge

"It is foolish and wrong to mourn
the men who died. Rather we should
thank God that such men lived."

US General George S. Patton

Airborne forces
Soldiers dropped into battle by parachute, or in gliders.

Allies
The countries that fought against Germany, Italy, and Japan in the war, including Britain, the United States, and the Soviet Union.

Annex
To take over territory bordering on your own country.

Appeasement
Term for the policy of the British government before World War II, based on giving Hitler what he wanted in order to "appease" him—make him peaceful.

Atom bomb
A very powerful type of bomb that releases the energy in atoms to create a massive explosion.

Axis powers
Countries belonging to the Axis alliance, chiefly Germany, Italy, and Japan.

The Blitz
The German bombing raids on British cities in 1940–41.

Blitzkreig
German word meaning "lightning war"—the tactics employed by the Germans to win quick victories.

Collaborator
Term for a person in German-occupied Europe who worked with the Nazis.

Communist
The Communist Party was the political party that ruled the Soviet Union. Communists in other countries wanted to create a similar government in their own lands.

Conscription
System that makes joining the armed forces, or doing war work, compulsory.

Convoy
In the naval war, a convoy was a number of merchant ships sailing together, guarded by warships.

Czechoslovakia
Country made up of what are now the Czech Republic and Slovakia.

Democracy
Political system in which people vote to elect the government and leaders.

Depression
The Great Depression, or simply the Depression, was a worldwide economic collapse in which many people lost their jobs.

Dictator
Individual who rules a country without allowing anyone to oppose them.

Dutch East Indies
Former name of what is now Indonesia when it was part of the Dutch Empire.

Evacuate
To take trapped soldiers to safety, usually by sea, or to remove civilians from cities to avoid bombing.

Evacuee
One of the people, mostly children, evacuated from Britain's cities during World War II.

Fascist
Italian dictator Mussolini called his political party the Fascist Party and his followers were known as Fascists. "Fascist" came to be used as a general term for all similar people and organizations—believers in the rule of a dictator and aggressive military action.

French Indochina
Former name of Vietnam, Cambodia, and Laos, when they were part of the French Empire.

Gestapo
The German secret police.

Ghetto
An area of a city where Jews were forced to live by the Nazis.

Government-in-exile
Term for governments set up, mostly in London, to represent German-occupied countries.

Guerrilla war
A war fought by people who are not part of regular uniformed armies and who use tactics such as ambush and sabotage.

The mass murder of the Jews and other minorities by the Nazis during World War II.

Incendiary bombs
Bombs designed to cause fires.

Intelligence
In war, intelligence is information about the enemy, gathered from all sources.

Kamikaze
Japanese word meaning "divine wind," used for pilots who acted as suicide bombers.

Luftwaffe
The German air force.

Nazis
Members of the National Socialist German Workers' Party—the Nazi Party for short—led by Adolf Hitler, which ruled Germany from 1933 to 1945.

Neutral
Term for a country that does not take part in a war.

Occupation
Sending in armed forces to control all, or part, of another country.

Occupied Europe
The parts of Europe controlled by the Germans and their allies in World War II.

OSS
Short for Office of Strategic Services, an American secret organization that sent agents into German-occupied Europe.

Panzers
German tanks and other armored vehicles.

Partisans
Resistance fighters who used guerrilla warfare tactics.

Pocket battleship
A German warship with powerful guns, but smaller than a normal battleship.

A soldier captured by the enemy.

Propaganda
Information, often distorted, intended to persuade people to support their government or the war effort.

Radar
A device used in World War II for spotting and tracking enemy aircraft or ships.

RAF
The Royal Air Force—the British air force.

Rationing
System for dividing up scarce food and other goods by allowing individuals a certain fixed amount each week or month.

Reichstag
The German parliament.

Reparations
Payments demanded of defeated Germany after World War I to compensate the victors.

Resistance
An organization set up to oppose Germany and it allies in countries they had occupied.

Sabotage
Deliberate damage to equipment or transport links, such as bridges and railroads.

Slavs
Term for the Russians, Poles, Czechs, Ukrainians, and other peoples of central and eastern Europe, who speak similar languages.

SOE
Short for Special Operations Executive, a British secret organization set up to send agents into German-occupied Europe.

Soviet Union
After the Russian Revolution of 1917, the Russian Empire was renamed the Union of Soviet Socialist Republics (USSR), or Soviet Union for short. The Soviet Union broke apart in 1991.

The initials SS stand for the German word *Schutzstaffen*, meaning "protection squad." The SS was originally Hitler's bodyguard, but it grew into a large organization responsible for the secret police, concentration camps, and the extermination of Jews.

Superpower
Term used after World War II for the United States and the Soviet Union, which were the two most powerful countries in the world.

U-boat
A German submarine.

V-1
A pilotless German flying bomb, the forerunner of today's Cruise missiles.

V-2
A German rocket weapon, the forerunner of today's space rockets.

Versailles Treaty
The peace treaty imposed on Germany at the end of World War I.

Vichy France
The area of France not occupied by German armed forces in June 1940. The French government there, which collaborated with the Nazis, was known as the Vichy government.

War bond
War bonds raised money to finance the war effort. Citizens bought war bonds from their government; the government paid the money back with interest after the war.

Yugoslavia
Country made up of what are now Serbia, Croatia, Bosnia and Herzegovina, Slovenia, Montenegro, and the Republic of Macedonia.

GLOSSARY

INDEX

189

INDEX

CREDITS

The publisher would like to thank the following for their kind permission to reproduce their photographs:

(Key: a-above; b-below/bottom; c-center; f-far; l-left; r-right; t-top)

1 Imperial War Museum: Mapham, J. (Sgt) (BU 6666). 2-3 Imperial War Museum (NYF 80381). 4-5 Imperial War Museum (NYF 58682). 6 Imperial War Museum: ((GR 530) l/2, (EA 22331) l/3, (NAM 236) l/6; Hoffmann, Heinrich (MH 11040) (l/1); Morris (Sgt) & Midley (Sgt) (BU 3813) (l/4); No. 16 Group RAF (C 4451) (l/5). 8-9 The Art Archive: John Meek. 10 Corbis: Bettmann (cb); Underwood & Underwood (cr). Imperial War Museum: Brooke, J.W. (Lt) (Q 5100) (t). 11 Alamy Images: Mary Evans Picture Library (tl). Corbis: Bettmann (bl, br). 12 The Art Archive: (cr). Corbis: Bettmann (tl, cl); EPA (bc). 13 akg-images: (tl). DK Images: Courtesy of the Michael Butler Collection (tc). Getty Images: Imagno (br). 14 Alamy Images: Popperfoto (b). The Art Archive: Gunshots (tr). Corbis: Bettmann (tc). Imperial War Museum: (HU 6301) (br). 16-17 Alamy Images: The Print Collector. 18 The Art Archive: Private Collection / Marc Charmet (c). Corbis: Hulton-Deutsch Collection (cl). DK Images: Judith Miller / Larry & Dianna Elman (bc). The Kobal Collection: Universal (tr). 19 akg-images: (tl). Getty Images: Hulton Archive (b). Imperial War Museum: Hoffmann, Heinrich (HU 3640) (ca). 20 Corbis: Bettmann (b); EFE (b). 21 The Art Archive: (cl); Dagli Orti (br). Corbis: Hulton-Deutsch Collection (br). 22 Alamy Images: Popperfoto (clb). Corbis: (tl); Hulton-Deutsch Collection (br). 23 Corbis: Bettmann (cr). Getty Images: Central Press (tr); Keystone (t); Time Life Pictures / Carl Mydans (b). 24 Corbis: Hulton-Deutsch Collection (br). Getty Images: Hulton Archive (tl); Time Life Pictures / Timepix / Hugo Jaeger (c). 25 akg-images: (cl). Alamy Images: Popperfoto (br). The Art Archive: Dagli Orti (tr). Imperial War Museum: (MH 2088) (tl). Corbis: Bettmann (bc, r). 26 Corbis: Bettmann (cra). Imperial War Museum (FRA 204717) (cl). 27 Alamy Images: Mary Evans Picture Library (c). The Art Archive: John Meek (tc). Corbis: Bettmann (cra); Hulton-Deutsch Collection (br). 28-29 akg-images. 30 Alamy Images: Popperfoto (b). Corbis: Hulton-Deutsch Collection (cl). Imperial War Museum: (GER 18) (cra). 31 akg-images: (tr). The Art Archive: Private Collection / Marc Charmet (bl). The Bridgeman Art Library: Private Collection / Archives Charmet (br). Getty Images: Time Life Pictures / Timepix / Hugo Jaeger (c). 32 The Art Archive: Private Collection / Archives Charmet (bl). Getty Images: General Photographic Agency (t). Imperial War Museum: Ministry of Information (D 2593) (crb). 33 The Art Archive: Private Collection (tr). Getty Images: Time Life Pictures / William Vandivert (cl). Imperial War Museum: Royal Navy (A 6) (b). War Office (H 476) (tl). 34 Alamy Images: Mary Evans Picture Library (cl). Imperial War Museum: (HU 55566) (bl); Royal Navy (A 42) (tr). 34-35 akg-images: Ullstein Bild (bc). 35 Alamy Images: Popperfoto (bc). Imperial War Museum: (MISC 17435) (br); Bridge, N.H. (HU 55640) (ca). 36 Getty Images: Hulton Archive (tl). Photo12.com: Collection Bernard Crochet (c). 37 Imperial War Museum: (HU 1135) (br); Crown Copyright / Artist: Charles Cundall R.A. (IWM ART LD 35) (bl); War Office (F4505) (t). 38-39 Imperial War Museum: War Office / Puttman (Mr) & Malindine (Mr). (H 1637) 40 akg-images: Jean-Pierre Verney (cra). Corbis: Bettmann (l). Imperial War Museum: Free French Collection (HU 55588) (br). 41 Alamy Images: Popperfoto (bl). Getty Images: Fox Photos / Marshall (br). Imperial War Museum: (HU 63611) (tr); Beaton, Cecil (MH 26392) (cl). 42 Imperial War Museum: (HU 49253) (t); No. 609 Squadron RAF (CH 1823) (br); Royal Air Force (CH 13680) (bl). 43 Getty Images: Time Life Pictures / William Vandivert (tr). Imperial War Museum: Brandt, Bill (D 1568) (bl); German Air Force (C 5422) (t); Ministry of Information (D 18096)(bc). 44-45 Imperial War Museum: German Air Force (C 5422). 46 Alamy Images: Photos 12 (bl). Corbis: Bettmann (tr). Getty Images: Keystone (c). Imperial War Museum: Tomlin, H.W. (Lt) (A 724) (tl). 47 Corbis: Hulton-Deutsch Collection (c): Swim Ink 2, LLC (br). Imperial War Museum: Horton (Capt) (H 12744) (bl). 48 Alamy Images: Mary Evans Picture Library (tc). Getty Images: Keystone (bl). Photo12.com: Collection Bernard Crochet (c). 49 Imperial War Museum: Keating, G. (Cpt) (t (E 6600), bl (E 1580)); Royal Air Force / Hensser,

H. (Mr) (CM 749) (br). 50 akg-images: (tl, b). 51 The Art Archive: (tl); Dagli Orti (br). 52 akg-images: Ullstein Bild (t). Getty Images: MPI (br). 53 Alamy Images: Mary Evans Plcture Library (cra). Corbis: Bettmann (bl). Getty Images: Laski Diffusion (tl). Imperial War Museum: Ministry of Information (P 233) (bl). 54-55 Alamy Images: The Print Collector. 56 DK Images: Imperial War Museum (br). Getty Images: Time Life Pictures / Pix Inc. (bl). Imperial War Museum: (HU 86369) (tl). 57 akg-images: (t, bl). Getty Images: Keystone (br). 58-59 Getty Images: Time & Life Pictures / Frank Scherschel. 60 Getty Images: Keystone (t). Wikipedia, The Free Encyclopedia: (bc). 61 akg-images: (tc). Corbis: Bettmann (tr). Getty Images: AFP (cl); Time & Life Pictures (b). 62 The Bridgeman Art Library: Private Collection / Peter Newark Military Pictures (tc). Corbis: Museum of Flight (c). Wikipedia, The Free Encyclopedia: Imperial Japanese Navy (tr). 63 Corbis: K.J. Historical (br). Imperial War Museum: (t (OEM 21469), cb (OEM 3605)). Courtesy of The Museum of World War II, Natick, Massachusetts: (clb). 64-65 Corbis: Bettmann. 66 akg-images: (bc). Alamy Images: Pictorial Press Ltd. (t). 67 Corbis: (tr); Bettmann (tc); K.J. Historical / David Pollack (cr). Getty Images: Time & Life Pictures / Dmitri Kessel (cl). Imperial War Museum: (NY 7343)(bc). 68 Alamy Images: Mary Evans Picture Library (br). Imperial War Museum: Cartwright (Lt Cmdr) (HU 2675) (cl). 68-69 Imperial War Museum: (HU 2780) (tc). 69 akg-images: Ullstein Bild (tr). Getty Images: Time & Life Pictures / Pictures Inc. (cr). Imperial War Museum: (HU 2781) (c). 70 Corbis: Bettmann (t). Imperial War Museum: (MH 28352) (bl). 71 Getty Images: Time & Life Pictures / George Rodger (bl). Imperial War Museum: (cla HU 4569), tr HU 43339); Crown Copyright / Artist: Leslie Cole (IWM ART LD 5620)(cr). 72-73 Imperial War Museum: (HU 43339). 74 Corbis: (br); Time & Life Pictures / US Navy (bl). Getty Images: Time Life Pictures / National Archives (tr) Imperial War Museum / US Navy / Edward Steichen (tr). 75 Corbis: (tl). Getty Images: Keystone (tr). Courtesy of US Navy: US National Archives (b). 76 The Bridgeman Art Library: Private Collection / Peter Newark Military Pictures (tl). Corbis: (br); Bettmann (cl). Imperial War Museum: Royal Navy (HU 69098) (b). Courtesy of US Navy: (tr). 78 Corbis: Hulton-Deutsch Collection (b). Getty Images: Time & Life Pictures / George Strock (tl). 79 The Art Archive: Dagli Orti / Domenica del Corriere (br). Corbis: Hulton-Deutsch Collection (tl). Getty Images: Time & Life Pictures / William Vandivert (tr). Imperial War Museum: No. 9 Army Film & Photographic Unit (IND 2917) (cl). 80-81 Imperial War Museum: Chetwyn (Lt) (NA 5107). 82 Corbis: Bettmann (bl). Getty Images: Time & Life Pictures / National Archives (cr). Library Of Congress, Washington, D.C.: Byrne, Thomas A. (tl). 83 Corbis: Bettmann (br). Library Of Congress, Washington, D.C.: Douglas Aircraft Photo from OWI (bl); Saint Louis Dispatch (br). 84-85 Corbis: Bettmann. 86 Alamy Images: Popperfoto (cl); Helene Rogers (tr). Imperial War Museum (D 8336) (c). 86-87 Imperial War Museum: Ministry of Information (D 23740) (bc). 87 Imperial War Museum: Ministry of Information (t (D 3170), br (D 23830)); US Army Signal Corps (EA 9010) (cr). 88 Corbis: (tl); Bettmann (bc). Imperial War Museum: Ministry of Information (TR 911) (bc); Royal Air Force / Devon (F/O) (CH 11926) (br). 89 akg-images: (bl, bc). Getty Images: Harold M. Lambert (t). Imperial War Museum: Royal Air Force / Daventry (F/O) (C 380) (br). 90 Imperial War Museum: Keating, G. (Cpt) (E 2301) (c); War Office / Chetwyn, L. (Lt) (TR 1394) (tl); Windows (Sgt) E 14775) (b). 91 Imperial War Museum: Keating (Cpt) (NA 2514) (cr); Royal Air Force (TR 978) (t); Royal Navy / Hudson, F.A. (Lt) (A 12649) (cl). 92 Corbis: Hulton-Deutsch Collection (br). Imperial War Museum: Stubbs (Sgt) (NA 4940) (bl). 93 akg-images: (tl). Imperial War Museum: Dawson (Sgt) (NA 11034) (cl); Menzies (Sgt) (NA 16116) (b); Royal Air Force / Baker (F/O) (C 4363) (tr). 94 akg-images: (tl). Imperial War Museum: (t (RUS 3699), br (HU 5131)). Wikipedia, The Free Encyclopedia: (bl). 95 akg-images: (tr). Imperial War Museum: Slava Katamidze Collection / G. Lipskerov (ca). 96 Alamy Images: Mary Evans Picture Library (tr, b). 97 akg-images: (br). Corbis: Bettmann (cr). Getty Images: Keystone (tr). Imperial War Museum: (RUS 1191) (br). 98 Alamy Images: INTERFOTO Pressebildagentur (bl). Imperial War Museum: (HU 40239) (br); Royal Navy / Coote, R.G. (Lt) (A 12883) (cl). 99 Imperial War Museum: (ZZZ 3130 C) (tl); Royal Air Force / Daventry, B.J. (Flt Lt) (CH 15302)(br); Royal Navy / Davies, F.A. (Lt) (A 15424) (cr); Royal Navy / McNeill, M.H.A. (Lt) (A 23959) (bl). 100 Getty Images: (tr). Imperial War Museum: (c (MH 27178), br (HU 16541)). 101 The Art Archive: (bl). Imperial War Museum: (OEM 5182) (br). Science & Society Picture Library: Bletchley Park Trust (t). 102 Alamy Images: Popperfoto (br). Corbis: Bettmann (c). Imperial War Museum: Royal

Air Force (TR 134) (tl). **103 Imperial War Museum:** (tr (IWM FLM 2363), b(HU 63075)); Royal Air Force (C 3677) (tl). **104-105 Imperial War Museum:** (COL 205). **106 Corbis:** Bettmann (t, bl). **Getty Images:** Keystone (crb). **107 Alamy Images:** Mary Evans Picture Library (crb). **Corbis:** (clb). **Getty Images:** LAPI / Roger Viollet (bc). **Imperial War Museum:** (HU 1761) (cla). **108 Corbis:** Bettmann (bc), Swim Ink 2, LLC (cl). **Photo12.com:** Keystone Pressedienst (crb). **108-109 akg-images:** Michael Teller (tc). **109 The Art Archive:** Culver Pictures (tr); National Archives, Washington D.C. (b). **Getty Images:** Anne Frank House, Amsterdam (cr). **110-111 The Art Archive:** National Archives, Washington D.C.. **112-113 Imperial War Museum:** (GER 133). **114 akg-images:** Ullstein Bild (bl). **Getty Images:** Keystone (br). **Imperial War Museum:** (HU 59359) (bl). **Wikipedia, The Free Encyclopedia:** (c). **115 Corbis:** Hulton-Deutsch Collection (br). **Getty Images:** Keystone (t). **Imperial War Museum:** Comite d'Histoire de la 2eme Guerre Mondiale (MH 11145) (clb). **116 Getty Images:** Time & Life Pictures / Pix Inc. (t). **Imperial War Museum:** (HU 20926)(crb). **117 Alamy Images:** Tim Gainey (br). **Corbis:** Bettmann (bl). **Imperial War Museum:** (tl (HU 20288), tr (HU 49533)). **118 akg-images:** (cr). **Alamy Images:** Pictorial Press Ltd (cl). **Corbis:** David J. & Janice L. Frent Collection (c). **119 Imperial War Museum:** (MH 1984) (tl); Lotzof, H. (Lt) (E 26615) (cr); Ministry of Information (D 1966) (cl); Royal Navy / Mason, H.A. (Lt) (A 14149) (c). **Imperial War Museum:** (tl (TR 207), bc (H 42531)). **120 Photo12.com:** Coll-DITE / USIS (cl). **121 Imperial War Museum:** (l (BU 1040), c (PL 25481), crb (HU 28594)); Royal Air Force (CL 1005) (tr). **122 Corbis:** (bl). **Getty Images:** Time & Life Pictures / US Army Air Force (cra). **Imperial War Museum:** Royal Navy / McNeill, M.H.A. (Lt) (A 23961) (tl). **123 Imperial War Museum:** (MH 3097)(cl); Handford (Lt) (B5144) (cr). **124-125 Imperial War Museum:** (MH 3097). **126-127 Imperial War Museum:** (EA 25636). **128 Corbis:** Bettmann (bc). **Getty Images:** Time & Life Pictures / Life Magazine / William Vandivert (tr). **Imperial War Museum:** (cl (IND 2237), cr (SE 7910)). **Corbis:** (cr). **129 akg-images:** Ullstein Bild (cl). **Corbis:** (tr). **Imperial War Museum:** (IND 4723) (b). **130 Imperial War Museum:** (t (NYP 29231), br (EN 19866)). **131 Corbis:** (cra). **Getty Images:** Time & Life Pictures / Life Magazine / Peter Stackpole (cl). **Imperial War Museum:** (NYF 30343) (tl). **Mary Evans Picture Library:** Rue des Archives (cl). Somos Primos (www. somosprimos.com): (cr). **132 Corbis:** Bettmann (c, br). **133 Corbis:** (br); Hulton-Deutsch Collection (crb). **Imperial War Museum:** (NYP 46105) (cr). **Photo12.com:** Collection Bernard Crochet (br). **134-135 Alamy Images:** INTERFOTO Pressebildagentur. **136 Corbis:** Bettmann (br). **Imperial War Museum:** (NYT 12797 E) (bl). **137 Corbis:** Bettmann (tl). **Getty Images:** Time & Life Pictures / Carl Mydans (tr). **Imperial War Museum:** (HU 66477) (ca); Midgley (Sgt) (BU 508) (b). **138 Getty Images:** Keystone (b). **Imperial War Museum:** (MH 2111 B) (tl). **139 akg-images:** (tl, cr, tr). **The Art Archive:** Marc Charmet (clb). **Photo12.com:** Keystone Pressedienst (br). **140 Corbis:** Bettmann (tl); DPA (br). **Imperial War Museum:** Ministry of Information (D 21213) (bl); Royal Air Force (CL 3433) (cl). **141 Alamy Images:** Popperfoto (b). **Corbis:** Philip Wallich (tl). **Imperial War Museum:** Ministry of Information (D 4054) (cra). **142 The Art Archive:** Musée des 2 Guerres Mondiales, Paris (c). **Imperial War Museum:** (MOI FLM 1536) (cl). **Library Of Congress, Washington, D.C.:** WPA Art Project (bl). **142-143 Imperial War Museum:** Royal Air Force (TR 1127) (tc). **143 akg-images:** British Lion / Album (cr). **The Art Archive:** German Poster Museum, Essen / Marc Charmet (cl). **Imperial War Museum:** Loughlin (Sgt) (HU 38756) (tr); Ministry of Information (P 552) (c). **144 Getty Images:** AFP (tr). **Photo12.com:** Ullstein Bild (br). **145 akg-images:** (tr); Benno Gantner (bc). **Imperial War Museum:** Morris (Sgt) (B5330) (tr); Smith, D.M. (Sgt) (c (BU 1163), bc (BU 1121)). **147 Corbis:** Bettmann (t). **Imperial War Museum:** (EA 49214) (c); Shaw (F/Sgt) (CL 2362) (cr); US Army Signal Corps (EA 48892) (bl). **148 Corbis:** (br). **Imperial War Museum:** (HU 44924) (t). **Photo12.com:** Oasis (tl). **149 Imperial War Museum:** Malindine (Cpt) (BU 3728) (tr). **Library Of Congress, Washington, D.C.:** (tl). **Photo12.com:** Ullstein Bild (b). **150 akg-images:** (b). **Alamy Images:** Popperfoto (tc). **Getty Images:** Time & Life Pictures / William Vandivert (cra). **151 Imperial War Museum:** (HU 50242) (tr); Malindine (Cpt) (BU 5207) (tl); US Signal Corps (EA 65796) (b). **152-153 Corbis:** Yevgeny Khaldei. **154 Corbis:** (br). **Wikipedia, The Free Encyclopedia:** US Army (bl). **154-155 Imperial War Museum:** (NYP 58330) (t). **155 Alamy Images:** Popperfoto (br). **Corbis:** (br). **Imperial War Museum:** (cl (NYF 70679), cr (NYP 77198)). **156-157 Alamy Images:** Michael Ventura. **158 Corbis:** (tr, b). **159 Corbis:** Yevgeny Khaldei (cr). **Getty Images:** The Bradbury Science Museum / Joe Raedle (tr). **Imperial War Museum:** (HU 53442) (cl); Lockeyear, W. (Cpt) (BU 9195) (bc). **160 Corbis:** EPA (cl). **Imperial War Museum:** (MH 29427) (bl). **Mary Evans Picture Library:** Rue des Archives (r). **161 Corbis:** (tc). **Getty Images:** Time & Life Pictures / John Florea (br). **Imperial War Museum:** US Army Signal Corps / Tonne, Fred (EA 75894) (cl). **162-163 Corbis:** EPA. **164-165 Photo12.com:** Oasis. **166-167 Imperial War Museum:** Tanner (Cpt) (TR 1802). **168 Getty Images:** Time & Life Pictures / Pat English (tr). **Imperial War Museum:** Royal Air Force / Devon, S.D. (Flt Lt) (CH 15115) (cl). **168-169 Imperial War Museum:** Christie, J. (Sgt) (BU 11357) (bc). **169 Alamy Images:** Popperfoto (bc). **Corbis:** Bettmann (cr). **Getty Images:** Harry Todd (tr). **Imperial War Museum:** (HU 69908) (tl). **170 Imperial War Museum:** Christie (Sgt) (BU 10264) (tr). **Photo12.com:** Oasis (b). **171 The Art Archive:** Domenica del Corriere / Dagli Orti (c). **Corbis:** (br). **Imperial War Museum:** Jones, A.H. (Sgt) (BU 9768) (tl). **172-173 Imperial War Museum:** (MH 24088). **174 akg-images:** (cl). **Alamy Images:** Popperfoto (br). **Getty Images:** Three Lions / Muras (tr). **175 Corbis:** Bettmann (tl, cl). **Imperial War Museum:** (HU 73010) (tr). **176 Getty Images:** Keystone (c); MPI (tl). **Photo12.com:** Xinhua (b). **177 The Bridgeman Art Library:** Private Collection / Peter Newark Military Pictures (c). **Getty Images:** AFP (br). **Imperial War Museum:** British Army Rifle Brigade / Godfray, Martin (Sgt) (KOR 604) (tr). **Photo12.com:** Oasis (tc). **178 Corbis:** Bettmann (tr); DPA (bl). **Getty Images:** Time & Life Pictures / George Skadding (c). **179 The Advertising Archives:** (tl). **Getty Images:** AFP / STF (cra). **180 Corbis:** Bettmann (tl). **Getty Images:** Evening Standard (crb). **Imperial War Museum:** Royal Navy (CT 121) (c). **181 Corbis:** Bettmann (cl). **Getty Images:** Tom Stoddart (b). **Magnum Photos:** Philip Jones Griffiths (tl). **Photo12.com:** Keystone Pressedienst (cra). **182 Corbis:** Reuters / Arnd Wiegmann (t). **Getty Images:** AFP / Toshifumi Kitamura (b). **183 Alamy Images:** Photos 12 (cra). **Corbis:** Peter Turnley (tl, b). **Getty Images:** AFP / Jiji Press (cl). **184-185 Alamy Images:** Richard Wareham Fotografie.

Jacket images: *Front:* **Corbis:** Bettmann. *Back:* **Getty Images:** National Geographic / Anthony Peritore. *Spine:* **Corbis:** Bettmann

All other images © Dorling Kindersley
For further information see: www.dkimages.com

Thanks to Marion Dent for proofreading and to Jackie Brind for indexing.

Thanks to Elizabeth Bowers, Jane Fish, and Abigail Ratcliffe at the Imperial War Museum, Vincent Marzello, and Heavy Entertainment.

The publisher wishes to acknowledge the following publications. Every effort has been made to contact the rights owners in each case but the publisher would welcome information on any omissions.
p45 *Waiting For the All Clear* edited by Ben Wicks (Bloomsbury) (t), Imperial War Museum Sound Archive: Stewart, Gwendoline (5334) (b), p110 *If This Is A Man* by Primo Levi (Jonathan Cape, reprinted by permission of The Random House Group Ltd), p124 *D-Day 1944* by Robin Neillands and Roderick de Normann (Weidenfeld and Nicolson, a division of the Orion Publishing Group, London, © Robin Neillands and Roderick de Normann 1993), p125 Imperial War Museum Sound Archive: Spearman, William (9796), p163 *Eye-Witness Hiroshima* edited by Adrian Weale (Constable & Robinson Ltd, Robinson © 1995) (t), p163 Jim Corley (b).

The publisher would like to thank the following for their kind permission to reproduce their photographs and footage on the DVD.
All footage © Imperial War Museum: A70 514/95+96 "Scenes at Auschwitz concentration camp, Poland", ADM 4 Why We Fight series "War Comes To America", ADM 7 Why We Fight series "Prelude to War", ADM 8 Why We Fight series "The Nazis Strike", ADM 9 Why We Fight series "Divide and Conquer", ADM 10 Why We Fight series "Battle of Britain", ADM 11 Why We Fight series "Battle of Russia", ADM 18 Why We Fight series "Battle of China", ADM 489 "The invasion of Iwo Jima...", ADM 2561/4 "ASDIC - Practical demonstration of an attack", ADM 555/01+02 "Captain Walker's Second Escort Group", ARY 3 "HMS Graph at Sea", AYY 31-32A "British Army record footage 1940", AYY 34-36 "British Army record footage 1940", AYY 38-39 "British Army record footage 1940", AYY 78 "City Fires – London and Manchester", AYY 18 "British Army record footage 1940", AYY 275 "British Army record footage 1942", COI 239 "From Italy to D-Day", COI 241 "From D-Day to Paris", COI 277 "From Paris to the Rhine", COI 246 "From The Rhine to Victory", COI 155 "Rationing in Britain", COI 426/2 "Coastal Command", COI 929 "We Sail At Midnight", COI 501 "Stalingrad", COI 177 "Berlin Airlift", COI 943 "London Can Take it", CVN 315 "Left of the Line", FOY 3 "The Nazi Plan – the Rise of the NSDAP", JYY 60+61 "Japanese capture of Singapore", MGH 246 "Westward Ho!", MGH 633 "Christmas Under Fire", OPX 236-239 "RAF record footage 1944", UKY 209 "The Front Line", UKY 268 "The Dawn Guard", UKY 302 "Britain's RAF". UKY 283 "Words for Battle", UKY 372 "Corvettes", UKY 576 "The Eighty Days", WIF 411 "Welt im Film – special report, the Berlin situation" 411, WPN 211 "War Pictorial News no 211", WPN 215 "War Pictorial News no 215", WPN 221 "War Pictorial News no 221", WPN 79 01 "War Pictorial News no 79", WPN 79 02 "War Pictorial News no 79", WPN 228 "War Pictorial News no 228", WIF 25-01 "Welt im Film no 25", WPN 275 "War Pictorial New no 275".
Images: **Imperial War Musem:** (HU 55523), **Alamy Images:** Richard Wareham Fotografie, **Getty Images:** Tom Stoddart.

CREDITS AND ACKNOWLEDGMENTS